# CONFLICTS AND TENSIONS IN ISLAMIC JURISPRUDENCE

*Publications of the Center for Middle Eastern Studies, Number 5*

WILLIAM R. POLK, GENERAL EDITOR

# CONFLICTS AND TENSIONS IN ISLAMIC JURISPRUDENCE

NOEL J. COULSON

THE UNIVERSITY OF CHICAGO PRESS
CHICAGO & LONDON

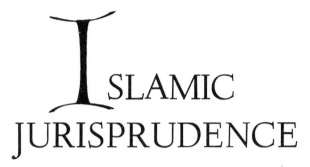

*Publications of the*
CENTER FOR MIDDLE EASTERN STUDIES

1. *Beginnings of Modernization in the Middle East: The Nineteenth Century*
   Edited by William R. Polk and Richard L. Chambers
2. *The Mosque in Early Ottoman Architecture*
   By Aptullah Kuran
3. *Economic Development and Regional Cooperation: Kuwait*
   By Ragaei El Mallakh
4. *Studies in the Social History of Modern Egypt*
   By Gabriel Baer
5. *Conflicts and Tensions in Islamic Jurisprudence*
   By Noel J. Coulson

*Library of Congress Catalog Card Number: 79–80433*

THE UNIVERSITY OF CHICAGO PRESS, CHICAGO 60637
The University of Chicago Press, Ltd., London W.C. 1


Published 1969

Printed in the United States of America

# CONTENTS



*General Editor's Foreword* vii

INTRODUCTION 1

1. REVELATION AND REASON 3

2. UNITY AND DIVERSITY 20

3. AUTHORITARIANISM AND LIBERALISM 40

4. IDEALISM AND REALISM 58

5. LAW AND MORALITY 77

6. STABILITY AND CHANGE 96

*Index* 117

# GENERAL EDITOR'S FOREWORD

The Center for Middle Eastern Studies at the University of Chicago was founded in October, 1965. The more than two dozen members of its faculty offer courses on subjects ranging from the geography of Morocco to the literature of Iran, and from the beginnings of the Muslim state in the time of Muhammed to contemporary political problems. The Center and the Oriental Institute, which deals with the more ancient periods of the Near East, enable the University to offer perhaps the most complete program on the Middle East available anywhere in the world.

It is the purpose of the Center to encourage and disseminate scholarly work on the Middle East. To this end, the Center provides fellowships and research funds and brings to the University visiting scholars. This book, the result of one such visit, is based on six lectures given at the University of Chicago Law School.

Professor Noel J. Coulson, Professor of Oriental Laws in the University of London, is one of the most eminent students of Islamic law in the world today. A barrister-at-law of Gray's Inn, he is the author of a history of Islamic law and was Dean of the law faculty of Ahmadu Bello University in Nigeria from 1965 to 1966.

## GENERAL EDITOR'S FOREWORD

Until recently, the field of Islamic jurisprudence has often been treated as an adjunct of Oriental studies with particular emphasis on textual criticism. Relatively few non-Islamic scholars have attempted to deal with Islamic law either to explain aspects of Islamic civilization or as a conceptualization of Islamic politics. In this volume, the fifth of a series of works published by the University of Chicago Press for the Center for Middle Eastern Studies, Professor Coulson probes the nature of Islamic law by examining six polarities: revelation and reason, unity and diversity, authority and liberty, idealism and realism, law and morality, and stability and change. Under these headings, Professor Coulson elucidates the development of Islamic law at the hands of judges and jurist consults. The book is the work of a lawyer thoroughly and deeply versed in his subject. It is of great value to students of society and politics as well as to those of comparative law.

This and forthcoming volumes in the series will illustrate the extent and diversity of the interests of the members at the Center for Middle Eastern Studies at The University of Chicago.

WILLIAM R. POLK
*Director of the Center for Middle Eastern Studies*

# INTRODUCTION

The conflicts and tensions of Western jurisprudence, as they are familiar to students of Western legal theory, stem from controversy on the fundamental question of the nature of law. They are essentially the product of diverse philosophies of life and political ideologies which have found their vogue in Western civilization and which differ in their view of the ultimate values and purposes of human life.

Those who would anticipate, or perhaps apprehend, that a discussion of the conflicts and tensions of Islamic jurisprudence must proceed on this same level and involve questions of the same order will, I fear, be disappointed or, alternatively, relieved. For Islamic jurisprudence, by definition, precludes any such basic conflicts of ideology. Islam means total submission and surrender to Allāh. It is therefore the will of the Muslim God, and that will alone, which determines the ultimate values and purposes of human life. The fundamental question of the nature of law is answered for Muslim jurisprudence, in terms that admit of no compromise, by the religious faith itself. Law is the divinely ordained system of God's commands. To deny this principle would be, in effect, to renounce the religious faith of Islam.

But while law in Islam may be God-given, it is man who must apply the law. God proposes: man disposes. And between the original divine proposition and the eventual human disposition is interposed an extensive field of intellectual activity and decision.

A Muslim court in Morocco today, for example, may grant a wife's petition for divorce on the ground that she has suffered harm as a result of her husband's taking a second wife. The decree of divorce is the human disposition which stems from the divine proposition contained in the Qur'ān that "wives should be treated with consideration." But between the Qur'ānic text and the court's decree lies a long series of questions. What establishes the authenticity of the Qur'ānic text? What is the precise significance, in terms of social behavior, of the norm that is contained therein? By what authority is that significance determined and expressed in the form of legal rules which a court of law must observe and legal remedies which it may provide? These and similar questions it was the task of Muslim jurisprudence to answer. In short, jurisprudence in Islam is the whole process of intellectual activity which ascertains and discovers the terms of the divine will and transforms them into a system of legally enforceable rights and duties. It is within, but only within, these strict terms of reference that the tensions and conflicts of Islamic legal thought arise.

The six principal tensions and conflicts that I propose to examine in this series of lectures must not be regarded as isolated and distinct aspects of Islamic legal thought, but as closely interrelated topics which often merge inextricably one into another. A consideration of them, as they have emerged from thirteen centuries of Islamic legal history will, I think, provide a sound basis for appreciating the major achievements and problems of contemporary law and jurisprudence in Islam.

# 1

# REVELATION AND REASON

Islamic law has been alternatively described as a divine law and as a jurists' law. These apparently contradictory descriptions reveal the basic tension that exists in the system between divine revelation and the human reasoning of jurists. In this first lecture, therefore, my inquiry concerns the respective roles played by these two distinct elements in the fashioning of Islamic law, and I shall not, at this point, take the inquiry beyond the traditional or classical jurisprudence of medieval times.

The comprehensive system of personal and public behavior which constitutes the Islamic religious law is known as the Sharīʿa. The goal of Muslim jurisprudence was to reach an understanding (*fiqh*) of the Sharīʿa. Its primary task, therefore, was to formulate the principles or sources (*uṣūl*) from which such an understanding might be achieved. Consequently, Muslim legal theory is known as *uṣūl al-fiqh*, or the "sources of understanding."

Clearly the primary source of such understanding will lie in what Islam accepts as divine revelation. In orthodox Islamic belief this is strictly confined to the revelations vouchsafed by Allāh to his chosen instrument the prophet Muḥammad. They appear in two forms: first, in the text of the Qur'ān, which is to the Muslim the very word of God himself; second, in the activities and the decisions of the Prophet as the ruler of the Muslim community, these extra-Qur'ānic precedents being known collectively as the Prophet's practice or *sunna*.

But the Qur'ān and the *sunna* taken together in no sense constitute a comprehensive code of law. The legal material they contain is a collection of piecemeal rulings on particular issues scattered over a wide variety of different topics; far from representing a substantial corpus juris, it hardly comprises the bare skeleton of a legal system.

The first 150 years of Islam were characterized by an almost untrammeled freedom of juristic reasoning in the solution of problems not specifically regulated by divine revelation. Such rules of law as the Qur'ān and the *sunna* established were regarded simply as ad hoc modifications of the existing customary law. This existing law remained the accepted standard of conduct unless it was expressly superseded in some particular by the dictates of divine revelation. And when new circumstances posed new problems, these were answered on the basis simply of what seemed the most proper solution to the individual judge or jurist concerned. In the expression of his personal opinion, known as *ra'y*, the individual was free to take into account any factors he deemed relevant. In short, in these early days law had a distinctly dual basis. It was a compound of the two separate spheres of the divine ordinance and the human decision.

But this pragmatic attitude soon fell victim to the increasing sophistication of theological and philosophical inquiry. Among the growing body of scholars whose deliberations were attempting to explain the essence of their faith arose a group who took their stand on the principle that every aspect of human behavior must of necessity be regulated by the divine will. In their philosophy of law the legal sovereignty of God was all-embracing. To allow human reason to formulate a legal rule – whether by continued recognition of a customary law or by juristic speculation on a new problem – was tantamount to heresy. In the language of Islamic theology it was "to set up a competitor with Allāh" and to contradict the fundamental doctrine of the omniscience and omnipotence of the Creator.

Because this group believed that every rule of law must be derived either from the Qur'ān or from the Prophet's practice as recorded in reports known as *ḥadīth*, they became known as "the supporters of *ḥadīth*" (*ahl al-ḥadīth*), as against "the supporters of *ra'y*" (*ahl al-ra'y*), who maintained that the free use of human reason to elaborate the law was both legitimate and necessary. The rift between the two groups hardened in the eighth century into the first fundamental conflict of principle in nascent Islamic jurisprudence and epitomized the tension between the divine and the human element in law.

The compromise formula in this conflict was devised

in the early years of the ninth century by the jurist Shāfiʿī, an achievement which gained for him the title of the "father of Muslim jurisprudence." On the one hand Shāfiʿī stood foursquare behind the principle of the divinely inspired *sunna* of the Prophet as recorded in the *ḥadīth*. On the other hand he acknowledged the necessity for human reason to provide legal rules for situations not expressly or specifically regulated by divine revelation. But this reason, he argued, could not be in the form of *ra'y*. Reason could not operate as a source of law independent of the divine will, to achieve whatever ends or purposes an individual jurist thought desirable. This would be to recognize a human legislative authority along with the divine. The ultimate goals and purposes of human behavior had been laid down by Allāh, and were desirable and right not because the human intellect could assess them to be such, but simply because Allāh had so ordained. The role of human reason must, therefore, be entirely subordinate to the principles established by divine revelation. Its function was simply to regulate new cases by applying to them the principles upon which the divine revelation had regulated similar or parallel cases. This process was known as reasoning by analogy, or *qiyās*. Since the process must find its starting point in an accepted manifestation of the divine will, human reason was harnessed to the implementation and development of the divine law and could not operate independently of it.

Shāfiʿī's thesis became the basis of the classical exposition of Islamic legal theory. From the tenth century onward the juristic consensus was that a rule of law must be derived either from the Qur'ān or the *sunna* or by analogical deduction therefrom. But by way of a postscript, classical legal theory recognized that in some cases strict analogical reasoning might entail injustice and that it was then permissible to use a more liberal form of reasoning. Although this came close to being the same thing as the *ra'y* of the ancients, it was now dressed up in more sophisticated terminology and called *istiḥsān* ("seeking the most equitable solution"), or *istiṣlāḥ* ("seeking the best solution for the general interest"). But this was no longer regarded, in theory, as giving human reason sovereign play. "Equity" and "the public interest" were now seen as the purposes of Allāh which it was the task of jurisprudence to implement in the absence of any more specific indication in the Qur'ān or the *sunna*. In sum, therefore, the classical legal theory expresses to perfection the notion of law as the comprehensive and preordained system of God's commands.

To illustrate the interaction of the two elements of divine revelation and human reason and the operation of the various juristic principles and methods of reasoning which I have now briefly outlined, I propose to consider one problem in some depth rather than several problems in what would necessarily be a superficial manner. The problem chosen is one of inheritance, and it is particularly appropriate for two reasons.

First, there is no topic in Islamic law of more pronouncedly individual characteristics than that of succession. The meticulous precision with which the priorities of the different legal heirs are determined, and the quantum of their entitlement defined, is regarded generally by Muslim scholars as the zenith of juristic achievement and the showpiece of the whole legal system. According to a famous dictum of the Prophet, the laws of inheritance constitute "half the sum of all useful human knowledge." Some may regard the subject as a labyrinth of legal complexity, but for all that, it remains a most typical expression of the spirit of Muslim legal thought.

Secondly, the laws of inheritance form a vital and integral part of the family law of Islam and in a sense may be said to constitute its focal point; for the system of priorities and the quantitative value set on the entitlement of each relative derives from the position which that relative occupies in the scheme of family ties and responsibilities. Rights of inheritance are the consideration for the duties owed to the deceased while he was alive. Hence the system mirrors the Islamic concept of social values and the structure of the family group.

The particular problem of inheritance which I have chosen is the case of a Muslim woman who dies intestate and is survived by her husband, her mother, her paternal grandfather, her germane brother and two uterine brothers. How will her estate be apportioned among these surviving relatives?

A few remarks by way of preliminary explanation. First, we must assume that all the preliminary issues involved in succession have been resolved and that it only remains to distribute the estate among the surviving relatives. We are not concerned with any distinction between movable and immovable property, between chattels and real estate. The inheritance is regarded at this stage as a single entity, and the only problem is to determine the rights of each relative therein in terms of a fractional share of quantitative value.

Secondly, in regard to the particular relatives involved in this case, the distinction between a germane brother, or brother of the full blood, and one of the half-blood is extremely relevant in the context of Islamic society. There is a relatively high incidence of the half-blood relationship – both the consanguine relationship of brothers who have the same father but different mothers, because of the institution of polygamy, and the uterine relationship of brothers who have the same mother but different fathers, because of the ease and frequency of divorce and the remarriage of divorced women.

Finally, this problem, as with many problems discussed in the traditional textbooks of Islamic law, did not arise as an actual case but as a hypothetical one. It bears the name of Mālik's Rule, after the jurist who devised the case and solved it. I have perhaps said sufficient already to indicate that Islamic law in its developed form is a jurists', rather than a judges' law. It was expressed in textbooks as the doctrine of the jurists, not in law reports containing the decisions of the judiciary. It was a system where the academic lawyer controlled the practicing lawyer, where the chair was not only more comfortable but more influential than the bench. Consequently the problems which exercised the minds of the jurists were problems of pure law. Unhappily, perhaps, the speculation of the Muslim jurists lacks the color of particular factual situations and human circumstances, which, to the Western student of law at any rate, often demonstrate that truth is infinitely stranger than fiction.

The first step in the solution of the present problem of succession was to consider whether there were any relevant rules in the Qur'ān on the subject. Although there are, perhaps, more Qur'ānic regulations on inheritance than on any other single legal topic, these regulations are in no sense comprehensive. In essence they prescribe fixed fractional portions of the estate as the entitlement of certain nominated relatives who, as a general rule, would never have been legal heirs under the customary law which prevailed in Arabia prior to the advent of Islam. In pre-Islamic Arabia, where the unit of society was the patrilineal and patriarchal tribe, succession was confined to male agnate relatives – a system designed simply to keep the tribal patrimony within the tribe. The heirs nominated by the Qur'ān are therefore females – the mother, the daughter and the sister; a non-agnatic male – the uterine brother; and the spouse relict – the surviving husband or wife. But what of the male agnate relatives who find scarcely any mention in the Qur'ān? And if their rights of succession had not been completely extinguished by the Qur'ānic legislation, how did they now stand in relation to the new heirs whose rights had been precisely fixed by the Qur'ān?

For the answer to this root problem, Muslim jurisprudence turns to the complementary material of divine revelation which lies in the *sunna* of the Prophet, and finds the solution in the Prophet's decision in the case of the estate of Sa'd.

Sa'd was a close companion and supporter of the

Prophet, who had met his death in one of the battles fought to establish the new religion. His widow complained to the Prophet that she and her two daughters were now left without any means of support as the whole of Sa'd's estate had been appropriated by his brother, who claimed the inheritance—quite properly under the customary tribal law—as the nearest male agnate. Shortly after this, according to the early commentators, "the Qur'ānic verses of inheritance were revealed"—a comment which is sufficient indication of the typically ad hoc nature of the Qur'ānic laws. The Prophet then ruled that Sa'd's widow should take from the estate her portion prescribed by the Qur'ān, namely one-eighth; that the two daughters should similarly take their prescribed portion, collectively two-thirds of the estate, and that Sa'd's brother was entitled to the residue, a share amounting to five twenty-fourths of the inheritance in this case.

This decision laid down what may fairly be termed the golden rule of the Islamic law of inheritance. The Qur'ānic heirs take their allotted portions as a first charge upon the estate, and the male agnate relatives then succeed to the residue. The Islamic law of inheritance thus rests upon a dual basis—the class of male agnate heirs whose rights derive from the pre-Islamic tribal law, and the class of Qur'ānic heirs whose rights were prescribed by the divine revelation. In other words, the customary law remained operative but was now subject to the modifications introduced by the Qur'ān. In inheritance, as in other spheres of law, the Qur'ān did not entirely supplant and supersede existing law, but merely reformed it in certain particulars.

The distribution of any estate under Islamic law must, therefore, depend upon the classification of the claimants either as Qur'ānic heirs or as residuaries. In our present case the husband, mother, and uterine brothers are Qur'ānic heirs, while the paternal grandfather and the germane brother are male agnate residuaries.

But this golden rule of distribution established by the Prophet's decision in Sa'd's Case is in fact, a secondary stage in the solution of a succession problem. It is clear that not every surviving relative of a deceased person, whether Qur'ānic heir or male agnate, can claim a share of the inheritance. The closeness or strength of relationship of one relative will put him in a superior position to other relatives. Rules of priority will serve to oust and exclude the weaker relationships so that the number of entitled claimants is reduced to manageable proportions. The primary task, therefore, is to determine which of the surviving relatives are entitled legal heirs. The rules of priority or exclusion which effect this owe very little to divine revelation—whether in the Qur'ān or the *sunna* of the Prophet—but derive almost entirely from the customary tribal law.

Roughly speaking, heirs fall into two groups with respect to priorities. A spouse, a child, or a parent is a primary heir and cannot be excluded from inheritance. More distant relatives are secondary heirs and may be excluded. But the overall cardinal principle is that only male agnates have the power to exclude other relatives from inheritance. The Qur'ānic heirs have no such power; they may be excluded themselves but can never exclude others. From this point of view they appear rather as supernumeraries. When they are not excluded from succession, they take their allotted portions and then leave the field to allow the real contest for succession to be fought out between the male agnates.

In our problem the husband and mother of the praepositus are primary heirs and cannot be excluded. On the other hand, no jurist doubted that the paternal grandfather, as an agnatic ascendant, was sufficiently superior to the maternal collaterals – the uterine brothers – to oust them from any right of succession. The only problem of priority, therefore, concerned the germane brother. Was he also to be excluded by the grandfather as an inferior agnate relative?

Juristic reasoning here started on the basis of the settled principle of customary law that the father of a deceased person ousts from succession the deceased's brother. From this some jurists derived the general principle that ascendants are a superior class of relatives to collaterals, and that therefore a grandfather, when he is the nearest surviving ascendant, takes the place of the father and, just as the latter would do, excludes the brother from succession. The majority view, however, laid emphasis not so much upon the class of relationship – ascendants or collaterals – but upon the degree of removal, from the praepositus, of the individual relatives concerned. Both the grandfather and the brother, it was argued, were at the second degree of removal from the praepositus, since there intervened between them and the praepositus the same common link, namely the father of the praepositus. And if class of relationship was to count as a secondary consideration, then it might be argued that it was the brother who had the stronger claim; for it was settled law that descendants as a class were superior to ascendants, so that it was the brother as the descendant of this common link (the praepositus' father), rather than the grandfather as the ascendant of it, who had the stronger tie with this common link and therefore, through it, with the praepositus himself. On these grounds the view prevailed that the grandfather did not exclude the germane brother but that both must rank on a parity as agnatic heirs.

Thus, from the Qur'ānic regulations and the Prophet's decision in Sa'd's Case, as supplemented by juristic reasoning based on the criteria of priority embedded in the customary law, emerges the systematic solution of the problem.

The uterine brothers are excluded by the grandfather. The husband takes his Qur'ānic portion of one-half and the mother her portion of one-sixth. The male agnates, the grandfather and the germane brother, stand on a parity and share the residue between them, each therefore receiving a share that amounts to one-sixth of the estate.

But now the inevitable discovery by the Muslim jurists, or at least of Mālik and his supporters, of the flaw in this solution. In the vein of hypothetical speculation to which Islamic jurisprudence is particularly prone, the question was put: "Suppose the grandfather had not survived the praepositus in this case? What then?" Then, in fact, the problem would have been identical with one which, it is recorded, some eight years after the death of the Prophet had confronted the then leader of the Muslim community, the Caliph Umar, and which acquired the celebrated title of "the Case of the Donkey" (*al-ḥimāriyya*). Though this was not a holy or binding precedent, since Umar could claim nothing of the Prophet's contact with the Divinity, the decisions of the Prophet's companions, like Umar, always had a persuasive authority.

Faced with the task of distributing an estate between the deceased's husband, mother, uterine brothers, and germane brothers, Umar first decided that the golden rule of distribution as enunciated by the Prophet should be applied systematically—the Qur'ānic heirs should take their allotted portions and then the male agnates should take the residue. The result was most unfortunate as far as the germane brothers were concerned; for there was here no superior heir to exclude the uterine brothers, who, as Qur'ānic heirs, were entitled to a portion of one-third as a first charge upon the estate. And this, together with the husband's portion of one-half and the mother's of one-sixth, completely exhausted the estate, so that nothing remained for the germane brothers to take as residue. Now since the rights of the husband and mother, as primary heirs, could not be disputed, the case amounted to a straightforward competition for the remaining one-third between the germane and the uterine brothers—in other words a head-on clash between the old tribal heirs, the germanes, and the new heirs introduced by the Qur'ān, the uterines. And the germanes, despite their traditional preeminence as agnatic heirs, had been totally vanquished and forced to vacate the field empty-handed, chagrined no doubt by the reflection that a few years earlier they would have been the sole legal heirs in this case.

The germane brothers, however, proved to be persistent litigants. On appeal to Umar they contended that while they sought no advantage vis à vis the uterines from their agnatic tie through the father of the praepositus, at least they ought not to be penalized because of it and come off worse than the uterines. Did not the deceased, the uterine brothers, and themselves all have the same mother—this being the sole ground of the uterines' claim? Why then should not they, as germanes, be allowed to ignore their agnatic tie and, basing their claim on the fact that they had the same mother, at least stand on a parity with the uterines? Umar accepted the validity of this argument, reversed his original decision, and ordered that the third of the estate remaining after the claims of the husband and mother were satisfied should go in equal shares to both the uterine and the germane brothers. The name of this case, "the Case of the Donkey," is derived from the way in which the germane brothers expressed their argument that they should be allowed to waive their agnatic tie and, discounting their father, inherit because of their maternal connection. "O Commander of the faithful," the common version of the case has them say, "suppose our father were a donkey of no account, do we not still have the same mother as the deceased?"

Umar's decision in the Donkey Case was a controversial one, and later jurisprudential debate upon it involved the whole question of the role of human reason in the elaboration of Islamic law. One side maintained that Umar's decision at first instance—the exclusion of the germanes from succession, was the more systematically sound and correct in principle. For them human reason was confined to the regulation of new cases strictly by analogy with established rules of divine origin. Here the relevant rule was the Prophet's decision in Sa'd's Case—that after the Qur'ānic heirs had taken their portions the male agnates succeeded to the residue. The germane brothers in the Donkey Case were male agnates. And once a male agnate, always a male agnate. As a title to inherit it was a permanent quality which could not be conveniently discarded in particular circumstances.

For the other side human reason was given freer rein. In particular cases strict analogy could occasion injustice, and it was then permissible to solve a problem on broad equitable considerations—this necessarily rather vague and ill-defined process being given the label of *istiḥsān*, or "equitable preference." For them Umar's final decision that the germanes should be allowed to inherit as uterines in these particular circumstances was an acceptable equitable modification of the strict rule of analogy that they should always and only inherit as male agnate residuaries.

Both sides, of course, were seeking justice in the individual case; and it was axiomatic that justice was identical with the terms of the religious law. The only question was what those terms were. It was a division of opinion among the jurists of Islam concerning the relative significance of the letter and the spirit of an established rule which seems not very far removed from the historical conflict in the English legal system between the champions of the strict letter of the common law and the advocates of equity.

To return now to our particular problem of succession: those jurists who accepted the principle underlying Umar's final decision in the Donkey Case maintained that this precedent governed the present case and therefore necessitated a revision of the systematic solution that the grandfather and the germane brother should share equally in the residue. If the grandfather were not present, they argued, the germane brother would not inherit as an agnatic brother but as a uterine brother. Why should this situation change simply because the grandfather comes upon the scene? And if the status of the germane brother remains that of a uterine when the grandfather does come upon the scene, then he must be excluded from succession, it being settled law that the grandfather excludes all uterines. In other words, why should the exclusion of the actual uterines by the grandfather not operate solely to his advantage? The germane brother did not exclude the uterines and would not inherit as an agnatic heir in the absence of the grandfather. Why, then, should he be allowed to do so simply because the grandfather is present, and to the latter's obvious detriment. Hence, the final solution of Mālik's Rule is to allow the grandfather to take the whole residue of one-third in these circumstances to the total exclusion of the germane brother.

My purpose here is simply to describe these juristic convolutions and not to criticize them. But the result is perhaps a little harsh on the hapless germane brothers. An equitable solution originally designed for their benefit is now systematically extended to their detriment. In the Donkey Case their father was deemed nonexistent, or at least asinine. Under Mālik's Rule their grandfather is now deemed nonexistent, or at least to have vanished temporarily, during an interim in which the brothers are deemed to have lost their agnatic tie. But the grandfather then reappears to exclude the brothers from inheritance and seize the whole residue of the estate. After this the germane brothers might well be in some confusion as to their precise status and identity.

This of course is only one example of the development of Islamic law through juristic speculation. But it is perhaps sufficient to show that in the fully fashioned fabric of the law the threads of divine revelation and human reason are so closely interwoven as to be almost inseparable. The reasoning of the Muslim jurists took many forms. It served to perpetuate standards of the preexisting customary law by formulating the proposition that divine revelation tacitly endorsed the customary law if it did not expressly reject it; analogy served to extend the specific rulings of divine revelation; "equitable preference" authorized departures from analogy to achieve a solution deemed more proper. But whatever form it took, juristic speculation in classical times was not regarded as an independent process which created a field of man-made law alongside the divine ordinances. It was entirely subordinate to the divine will in the sense that its function was to seek the comprehension and the implementation of the purposes of Allāh for Muslim society. Such conflicts regarding the province and the role of reason as there were in traditional jurisprudence concerned only the means by which this end might be achieved. In this light Islamic law is both a divine law and a jurists' law. In the contemplation of Islamic jurisprudence these two descriptions are complementary and not contradictory.

# 2

# UNITY AND DIVERSITY

"Difference of opinion within my community is a sign of the bounty of Allāh." This alleged dictum of the Prophet Muḥammad serves to explain and justify, to Muslim jurisprudence, the phenomenon of the widespread divergence in the doctrines of the jurists qualified to expound Sharī'a law. In a sense the tension between unity and diversity in Islamic legal doctrine is a natural and inevitable consequence of the basic tension I spoke of in the previous lecture between the two constituent elements of Islamic law: for divine revelation represents the fixed and constant factor, and human reason the variable and fluctuating factor, in Islamic jurisprudence. There is also involved in the present antinomy the distinction between the ideal and the actual state of affairs. Muslim jurisprudence, at least in its classical form, had no doubt that Sharī'a law existed as a single comprehensive and uniform code of behavior prescribed by Allāh for all his creatures on earth. But in its endeavor to perceive and comprehend this ideal law the human intellect was fallible and deficient, and variation in the results of juristic speculation as to the contents of the Sharī'a had perforce to be accepted as a matter of fact. In much the same way Islamic political theory rested upon the ideal of a universal Muslim community or *'umma*, united under a single ruler or Caliph, while in historical reality Islam has been divided into a variety of politically independent states. Arising as it does out of the search to discover the ideal law of the Sharī'a, the phenomenon of unity and diversity in legal doctrine goes to the very heart of Muslim jurisprudence. There is an old Arab proverb to express this. "The person who does not understand divergence in doctrine," it runs, "has not caught the true scent of jurisprudence." (*Man lā ya'raf al-ikhtilāf lam yashumma rā'iḥata 'l-fiqh*).

Divergence of legal doctrine, as far as Sunnī Islam is concerned, is crystalized in the existence of four different schools or versions of Sharī'a law. Basically these schools were formed through the personal allegiance of groups of jurists to a founder-scholar from whom they derived their names of Ḥanafīs, Mālikīs, Shāfi'īs and Ḥanbalīs; but each school had its own peculiar circumstances of origin. The two oldest schools are the Ḥanafīs and Mālikīs, and both came into existence as the representatives of the legal tradition of a particular geographical locality—the former being the disciples of Abū Ḥanīfa (d. 767) in the Iraqi center of Kufa, the latter the followers of Mālik b. Anas (d. 796) in the Arabian center of Medina. This early period of Islamic jurisprudence, as I observed in the previous lecture, was characterized by an uninhibited use of personal reasoning (*ra'y*) to regulate cases not specifically governed by a text of the Qur'ān or a decision of the Prophet, so that Mālikī and Ḥanafī doctrines, naturally enough, diverged insofar as they rested upon and reflected the particular social traditions and environment of the two different localities. In contrast to the local character of these two early schools, the later schools of the Shāfi'īs and Ḥanbalīs were both born out of the jurisprudential controversy which arose during the ninth century on the subject of the sources of the religious law. The disciples of Shāfi'ī, who first formulated the systematic theory of law being derived from the Qur'ān, the *sunna* and reasoning by analogy, formed, after his death in 820, the Shāfi'ī school. Some thirty years later a group of scholars under the leadership of Aḥmad b. Ḥanbal (d. 855) formed the Ḥanbalī school. They stood four-square behind the principle of the paramount authority of the Prophet's *sunna*, which, they maintained, was being undermined by the forms of juristic reasoning recognized in the other schools.

By the end of the ninth century, however, the four schools had all come to subscribe to a basically common theory of the sources of law. And with their resulting recognition of a common purpose, initial rivalries gradually gave way to a state of peaceful co-existence. The original distinctions of geographical locality or juristic principle faded into obscurity, and the schools mutually regarded their several bodies of doctrine as equally legitimate attempts to define Allāh's law, equally authoritative versions of the Sharī'a.

What made this state of harmony possible was, essentially, the doctrine of consensus or *ijmā'*. This doctrine of consensus represents the paramount criterion of legal authority for Islam and shores up the whole structure of legal theory. It is the principle that the unanimous agreement of the qualified jurists on a given point has a binding and absolute authority. The whole process of Muslim jurisprudence, from the definition of the sources of law to the derivation of substantive rules therefrom, was a speculative effort of the human intellect. And it was the *ijmāʿ*, and the *ijmāʿ* alone, which gave the necessary authority to this process. For, in the ultimate analysis, it was the *ijmāʿ* which guaranteed the authenticity of the Qur'ān and the *sunna* as the material of divine revelation, and the validity of the method of reasoning by analogy to elaborate and extend the principles embodied in the divine revelation. But the conclusion that an individual jurist might reach, in terms of a substantive doctrine derived from the recognized sources, was in the nature of a conjecture. Whether he was deciding upon the precise meaning of a Qur'ānic text or resolving a novel problem, his conclusion could only amount to a tentative, or probable, statement of the divine law. But where the rule concerned was the subject of a general consensus, then its status was transformed into that of a certain and incontrovertible statement of the divine law; for the consensus was infallible. Muslim jurisprudence expresses the distinction in terms of knowledge (*ʿilm*) and conjecture (*ẓann*). Certain "knowledge" of the rules of the divine law could only come about where there was unanimity of opinion; the rest was "conjecture," which necessarily involved the recognition of variant opinions. Thus the *ijmāʿ* provides an umbrella authority for the variant doctrines of the different schools of law. Where the Muslim jurists could not agree, they agreed to differ. It is a candidly pluralistic philosophy of law, which recognizes that no individual opinion can claim, as against other variants, a unique authority. A phrase that occurs *passim* in Muslim legal literature epitomises this philosophy. Discussion of a controversial problem and an assessment of the various possibilities often ends with the words: "but Allāh alone really knows."

Legal theory thus endeavored to assert the fundamental unity of law in Islam by regarding the four schools as equally authoritative and blending them together as manifestations of the same single essence. But in legal practice the boundaries between the schools were firmly drawn. Each school came to have, in geographical terms, a settled sphere of influence inasmuch as the courts of a given area consistently applied its doctrines. Thus, broadly speaking, Ḥanafī law has traditionally been applied in that area of the Middle East now covered by Turkey, Syria, Lebanon, Iraq, Jordan, Egypt, and the Sudan, and in the Indian subcontinent. Mālikī law has governed the Muslim populations in North, West, and Central Africa. Shāfiʿī law has prevailed in East Africa, the southern part of the Arabian peninsula and in Southeast Asia. Ḥanbalī law is today the law of the land in the kingdom of Saudi Arabia. Moreover, under its doctrine of the mutual orthodoxy of the schools, legal theory tended to emphasize their common law and minimize their divergence. It created an impression that the schools spoke with one voice on all fundamentals and only differed on minor issues. But in fact the division between the schools in matters of substantive law goes deeper than this. Each school represents a cohesive system of law which has its own distinctly individual characteristics in terms of social values and juristic principles. This may become apparent from a consideration of the extent to which the doctrines of the schools coincide or diverge in certain aspects of matrimonial law.

Upon the essential nature of the institution of marriage all schools are in agreement. Marriage is a contract, concluded simply by the mutual agreement of the parties, under which the husband obtains the right of sexual union in consideration of the dower that he pays to the wife. All schools, too, recognize the institution of marriage-guardianship, under which the father or other close male relative of a girl has a measure of control over the marriage of his ward. But in regard to the important question of the extent of the guardian's powers, which is allied to the question of the legal capacity of the female ward, there is a clear distinction between the doctrine of the Sunnī majority on the one hand and the Ḥanafī school on the other.

Ḥanafī law puts male and female basically on the same footing with respect to their legal capacity to conclude transactions. Legal majority comes with the fact of physical puberty, when it is presumed, unless there is evidence to the contrary, that the person concerned has attained that degree of sound and mature judgment which enables him or her properly to manage his or her own affairs. Such a person of sound judgment is termed, in the language of the law, *rāshid*. Physical puberty is a matter to be established by appropriate evidence, but the law presumes that it cannot occur before the age of nine in the case of girls and twelve in the case of boys, and that it must have occurred by the age of fifteen for both sexes. Accordingly, at the outside limit of the age of fifteen, a girl is emancipated from her guardian's control, as being now *rāshid.* During her minority her guardian's control over her person and property includes his power to conclude a marriage contract on her behalf, but when she becomes adult she is perfectly free, inter alia, to conclude her own marriage contract without the intervention of the guardian.

According to the other Sunnī schools, however, no woman can conclude her own marriage contract. Her proper guardian must conclude the contract on her behalf; otherwise the purported marriage is a total nullity. Furthermore, even an adult girl may be validly contracted in her first marriage by her father, regardless of her own wishes in the matter. Only when she has been married before is her consent to her marriage necessary. This majority view, therefore, rests upon the principle that a female's person and property are subject to her guardian's control until she marries. Only then does she acquire a capacity to deal with her own property, and only after this will her consent to any other future marriage become relevant. In some mysterious way the quality of being *rāshid,* of having that mature judgment which is the point of emancipation, is acquired by a female through the sexual experience of her marriage.

But whether her consent to her marriage is required or not, the contract itself must always be concluded by her guardian. This point of Islamic law came in for discussion in the rather improbable setting of a libel action in the English High Court, in the case of *Saleh* v. *Od-*

*hams Press*, 1963.[1] The Muslim plaintiff complained that he had been held up to ridicule and contempt by an article that appeared in the defendant's newspaper under the heading "Child wife bought for £800," which went on to describe the plaintiff's marriage, concluded under the Islamic law of the Mālikī school with a Moroccan girl in Casablanca, in terms of a purchase – the sum of £800 apparently being arrived at by adding the cost of the plaintiff's air fare from England to Morocco to the amount of the dower he had paid in consideration of marriage. The defendants pleaded that they were justified in describing the marriage as a sale because the negotiations for marriage had been concluded between the plaintiff and the girl's uncle and because a sum of money was involved. But this plea failed. It was held that the defendants had grossly misrepresented the nature of the proceedings involved in a Muslim marriage. The marriage guardian, in this case the bride's uncle, was in no sense acting as a vendor. It was not he, but the bride herself, who received the dower, and he had concluded the contract, as the bride's representative and acting upon her wishes, because Mālikī law required him to do so. Accordingly the defendants were held liable in damages for libel.

The difference between the schools on the subject of marriage guardianship and woman's legal capacity in general is formally attributed, by classical jurisprudence, to divergent views on the authority and interpretation of certain alleged precedents of the Prophet. But in fact the difference has its roots in the circum-

1. Law Report in *The Times* (London), 25 June, 1963.

stances of origin of the two earliest schools of law, the Mālikīs and the Ḥanafīs. Mālikī law developed in the traditionally Arab center of Medina. The social standards it accepted and reflected were naturally those of the patriarchal Arabian tribe in which, inter alia, the male members of the tribe controlled the marriages of its women. Ḥanafī law, on the other hand, grew up in the Iraqi locality of Kufa, where Persian influence predominated (Abū Ḥanīfa himself was of Persian extraction) and where society, in contrast to that of Medina, was almost cosmopolitan. In this setting, where the traditional standards of Arabian tribal life had not the same relevance, it was natural that woman should have a relatively higher status and, in particular, the right to contract her own marriage.

From this example of a divergence in law which arose from different social environments, I turn to a sphere of the law where the schools are divided upon a matter of juristic principle. The subject involved is the marital relationship. The basis of the marital relationship, according to all the schools, might be summarized as the wife's duty to obey her husband and her right, in consideration of this, to maintenance and support from him. Nor is there any dispute among the schools on such fundamentals as the institution of polygamy—the husband's right to marry additional wives up to the permissible maximum of four concurrently. But, granted that the normal legal incidents of the marital relationship are the same for all the schools, the question arises: How far are the spouses free to regulate their own marital relationship, in terms of their rights and duties, by agreeing upon special terms or conditions in the marriage contract?

It was common ground that the spouses could not agree to something contrary to the essence of marriage. For example, it is of the essence of marriage that it is, in the initial intention of the parties at any rate, a lifelong union. Any agreement, therefore, which purported to set a time limit to the marriage would be a complete nullity. It was equally common ground that an agreement between the parties which served to buttress or reinforce the normal incidents of marriage was a valid and enforceable agreement. Such, for example, is the case of an agreement which specifies the amount of dower payable or fixes the sum of maintenance which the husband is to provide. But controversy arose between the schools as to terms and conditions which fell between these two extremes, which neither reinforced the normal incidents of marriage nor were contrary to the essence of marriage, but which attempted to modify or contradict the normal incidents of marriage. Suppose, for example, that upon the insistence of his bride a husband agrees in the marriage contract that he will not take a second wife during the continuance of their marriage. Is this a valid and enforceable agreement or is it not?

The basic juristic issue involved here is the principle known in Arabic legal terminology as *ibāḥa,* which may be translated as "tolerance." It refers to the "tolerance" of the lawgiver, Allāh, who allows his creatures on earth freedom of action and behavior outside the area covered by his specific commands or prohibitions. The question, therefore, in the context of our present problem, is whether or not the principle of *ibāḥa* can apply to allow the spouses freedom to determine that their marriage will be monogamous.

The majority view of the Ḥanafī, Mālikī, and Shāfiʿī schools is that *ibāḥa* has no relevance here. The necessary effects of a marriage contract, in terms of the rights and duties of the spouses, are specified by the divine law, binding upon the parties and not susceptible to variation by them at will. Hence an agreement by a husband not to exercise his established right of polygamy is a nullity. Despite the term in the marriage contract he may take a second wife, and the first wife has no legal remedy.

Ḥanbalī law, however, holds that the principle of *ibāḥa* does apply to this case. Agreements in general are valid and enforceable provided they are not in themselves specifically forbidden by the law or manifestly contrary to the essence of marriage. The rule of polygamy is permissive, not mandatory. It is not specifically forbidden nor is it contrary to the essence of marriage that a man should have only one wife. Hence the spouses' agreement in this regard is valid and enforceable. It is not enforceable, however, in the sense that the husband will be prevented from taking a second wife; but if he does, he will be in fundamental breach of his contract, so that the wife will be released from her own obligations thereunder and will obtain a decree of dissolution of her marriage on petition to the court.

The differences between the Sunnī schools on the two matters we have just considered can hardly be accounted trivial. At the same time the extent of their agreement can best be appreciated when Sunnī law as a whole is compared with the law of the minority Muslim sect of the Shīʿa, which today has its center in Iran, though there are also considerable numbers of Shīʿī Muslims in India, East Africa, and Iraq. For although Shīʿī law rests on the same material sources of the Qur'ān and the *sunna*, it often diverges from Sunnī law in a fundamental way. Shīʿī law, for example, recognizes as valid the institution of temporary marriage, or *mutʿa*, under which the wife agrees to cohabit with the husband for a fixed period of time in return for a fixed remuneration, called the "hire price" (*ujra*). In Sunnī jurisdictions such a temporary union would not only be void at civil law; it might amount to the criminal offence of illegal sexual union, carrying, traditionally, a minimum penalty of one hundred lashes and one year's imprisonment and a maximum penalty of death by stoning.

But perhaps the most outstanding rift between the two groups lies in their respective schemes of inheritance. This was the result of a fundamentally different approach toward the nature of the Qur'ānic legislation. Sunnī jurisprudence regarded the Qur'ānic rules as reforming the existing customary law in a number of particulars, so that in the absence of any specific modification the customary law was deemed to be still operative. In the contemplation of the Sunnīs, where the Qur'ān did not expressly reject a customary rule, it tacitly ratified it. The result of this approach was, as I observed in the previous lecture, that the Sunnī law of succession gives pride of place to the tribal heirs of the customary law, the male agnate relatives of the deceased. The women to whom the Qur'ān gave rights of inheritance for the first time are entitled, in appropriate circumstances, to the fractional portion of the estate which the Qur'ān allots to them. But where a male agnate relative of the deceased survives, this will be the limit of their entitlement. The male agnate, however distant a relative he might be, will step in and claim the residue of the estate; for the female, however close a relative she might be, does not have the status to exclude him from succession. Hence, if a Sunnī Muslim dies intestate, survived by a daughter and a distant male agnatic cousin, the daughter will be restricted to a portion of one-half of her father's estate, and the cousin will inherit the remaining one-half as residuary heir.

For the Shī'a, however, the Qur'ānic legislation was far from being merely a series of piecemeal reforms. They maintained that the Qur'ān laid down the basic elements of an entirely novel legal system, including a system of succession. It obliterated completely the preexisting customary law. Any rule of the customary law which was not expressly ratified by the Qur'ān was tacitly rejected. And therefore, because the Qur'ān nowhere expressly ratifies the preeminent claims of the male agnates, as such, to inheritance, they have no privileged position in the Shī'ī scheme of succession. One of the Shī'ī leaders is supposed to have expressed this principle in no uncertain terms. "As for the male agnates," he declared, "dust in their teeth." On this basis Shī'ī law marshals all relatives, male and female, agnate and otherwise, into a single comprehensive scheme of priorities based exclusively upon the nearness of their relationship with the deceased. Within this scheme any descendant of the deceased, male or female, has absolute priority over any collateral; so that the daughter of a deceased Shīʿī Muslim will totally exclude his brother, and, a fortiori, any more distant male agnate such as a cousin, from succession, and will inherit the whole of her father's estate.

The Islamic legal system of medieval or classical times, then, was a highly diversified system. There was a clear-cut ideological rift between the majority of the Sunnīs and the minority sect of the Shīʿa. And within Sunnī Islam the boundary lines between the four schools, in terms of both their substantive doctrine and the geographical areas of their application, were firmly drawn. From late medieval times onward, however, the dividing lines have been progressively relaxed, until today, in the legal practice of the countries of the Near and Middle East, they have almost totally disappeared.

The initial impetus in this process was provided by the work of legal scholars who devoted themselves to a study of the whole phenomenon of diversity of legal doctrine. One of the most notable scholars who broke out from the confines of the doctrine of his own school was the Ḥanbalī jurist Ibn Qudāma. In his magnum opus, entitled the *Mughnī*, Ibn Qudāma scrutinizes the views of the different schools and jurists and compares them with traditional Ḥanbalī doctrine. And although he betrays a natural personal allegiance to the doctrines of the founder of his school, Aḥmad b. Ḥanbal, he does not hesitate to assert the relatively superior merit of a variant doctrine when it appears to him to be the juristically sounder opinion. It is from works such as this of Ibn Qudāma, which stimulated the analysis of variant doctrines and an assessment of the grounds upon which they rested, that Islamic law takes on the appearance of a built-in comparative legal system.

Legal scholarship further reduced the tension between the schools by insisting that each individual Muslim was absolutely free to follow the school of his choice and that any Muslim tribunal was bound to apply the law of the school to which the individual litigant belonged. Not only this, but it was generally admitted that an individual had the right to change his school of law on a particular issue. "No one," wrote Ibn Taymiyya, another Ḥanbalī scholar of an independent turn of mind, "is obliged to follow any particular authority, except the Prophet himself, in everything he is allowed or forbidden to do. Muslims have never ceased to ask the advice of scholars, and to follow this authority on one occasion and that authority on another. If a person follows a particular authority on a specific issue because he thinks that this authority is most beneficial to him in his religion, or because he thinks his argument is the better one, or for any similar reason, this is permissible according to the great majority of Muslim scholars. This was not denied by Abū Ḥanīfa, Mālik, Shāfiʿī, Aḥmad b. Ḥanbal or anyone else."[2]

Although the jurists maintained that such a change of school must rest on the bona fide belief that the doctrine of the alternative school was intrinsically sounder, and could not be grounded purely on personal convenience, this proviso does not seem to have troubled unduly the Muslim courts of India and Singapore. Here, for example, an interesting series of judicial decisions has al-

2. *Majmū ʿa fatāwā*, 2:387.

lowed Shāfi'ī girls (Shāfi'ī being the traditional school of persuasion in Ceylon and Malaya) to benefit from a rule of Ḥanafī law on a specific matrimonial issue. The series began with the Bombay High Court case of *Muhammad Ibrahim* v. *Ghulam Ahmad*, 1864. A Shāfi'ī father petitioned the court to annul the marriage of his daughter on the ground that it had been contracted without his permission or intervention. Shāfi'ī law does in fact allow annulment in such cases. But the daughter claimed that she had contracted the marriage as a Ḥanafī, which school, as I have already observed, grants an adult woman full legal capacity in this regard. The court, on this ground, rejected the petition for annulment and held the marriage to be valid. It is difficult to say how far this case and its successors go; but it would seem that the decisions were based upon the equitable expedient of allowing a Shāfi'ī girl to avail herself of a more convenient rule of the Ḥanafī school, rather than on the firm principle that the girls concerned had become Ḥanafīs for all purposes.

It is against this background of the growing recognition, by jurisprudence and by legal practice, of the variant doctrines of the different schools as equally authoritative alternatives, that the most recent developments in the Muslim countries of the Near and Middle East must be viewed. During the last few decades codifications of Islamic family law have appeared in most of these countries, and one of the most striking features of the codes is the extent to which they represent a synthesis of the variant doctrines of the different schools. The principle underlying the codes is that the political authority has the power, in the interests of uniformity, to choose one rule from among equally authoritative variants and to order the courts of his jurisdiction to apply that rule to the exclusion of all others; and the choice of this rule or that has been made simply on grounds of social desirability, the codes embodying those variants which were deemed most suited to the present standards and circumstances of the community.

One of the most obvious trends in contemporary Middle Eastern society is the emancipation of women, and much of the substance of the codes is directed toward the improvement of their legal status. Thus, in the Mālikī country of Tunisia, girls are no longer subject to the strictures of the Mālikī law of marriage guardianship, since the Tunisian *Code of Personal Status, 1957*, adopts the Ḥanafī rule that an adult woman has a full legal capacity to conclude her own marriage contract. On the other hand, in the Ḥanafī country of Syria, wives no longer suffer from the traditional Ḥanafī doctrine which did not recognize any ground upon which an ill-treated wife might petition the court for divorce; for in 1953, the *Syrian Law of Personal Status* adopted the more liberal Mālikī law that a wife may petition for divorce on such grounds as the husband's cruelty, desertion, or failure to maintain her. Finally, both Mālikī wives in Tunisia and Ḥanafī wives in Syria now benefit from the more liberal Ḥanbalī doctrine relating to terms and conditions in marriage contracts which the codes of both these countries have now adopted. Previously, any agreement which the husband may have entered into and which was designed to safeguard the wife's position—such as an agreement that the husband would not take a second wife, or that the wife should be free to follow a professional career or social activities of her own choosing—could be broken by the husband with impunity. Now, however, in the event of the husband's breach of such an agreement, the wife will at least have the remedy of judicial dissolution of the marriage.

But what is perhaps the most intriguing instance of this process of selection from variant doctrines is to be found in the Law of Personal Status currently applicable in Iraq. I have noted the fundamental nature of the divergence that separates the Sunnīs as a whole from the sect of the Shī'a on the subject of inheritance. An Iraqi law of 1963 enacted that the basic Shī'ī system of succession was henceforth to apply to the estates of all Iraqi nationals.

There were indeed, sound social reasons behind this reform. The Sunnī law of inheritance, with its emphasis upon the rights of male agnates, caters for a tribal system of society. But in contemporary Iraq, particularly in urban areas, tribal ties have disintegrated, and the unit of society has become the more immediate family circle of parents and their issue, within which circle the female has an increasingly responsible role. The Shī'ī system of inheritance, on the other hand, consistently emphasizes the claims of this smaller family circle and gives females an important position within it, particularly in the rule, which I have already mentioned, that a daughter, or indeed any female descendant of the deceased, totally excludes the brothers or more distant male agnate relatives of the deceased from inheritance.

It may be, too, that in the particular context of Iraqi society such a transition from Sunnī to Shī'ī law was not difficult to accept, since the population of Iraq is approximately half Sunnī and half Shīʿī. Indeed, it is said that prior to the enactment of the Law of Personal Status, Sunnī Muslims who were in the twilight of their years and without male issue often professed conversion to the Shīʿī credo simply to prevent the bulk of their estate passing into the hands of some distant male agnate relative, whose very existence was a matter of indifference to them. Even so, the new Iraqi law of succession represents the first occasion on which the principle of selection has so decisively jumped across the traditional chasm between orthodox and sectarian Islam, to impose Shīʿī law upon a Sunnī population.

Today, then, within the national boundaries of the Muslim countries of the Near and Middle East there is greater unity in the law than there was in times past. Uniformity is, of course, one of the principal goals of codification of the law, and this has been, in large measure, achieved in Islamic family law, since the courts are bound by the terms of the national code and no longer have the power to choose between the variant doctrines of the school as recorded in the traditional authorities. Nor can they any longer apply to particular litigants the law of another school to which they might profess to belong, since the codes apply to all nationals regardless of particular religious allegiance.

From an international standpoint, however, the process has brought about a growing diversity in Islamic law. Under the principle of selection from doctrines of the different schools, the authors of the codes ranged freely over the whole vast corpus of traditional doctrine and chose therefrom those provisions which were deemed most suitable for their national society. A population previously governed by Ḥanafī law now found itself subject to an amalgam of the law of all the four Sunnī schools. Since, however, needs and circumstances vary from country to country, this modern process of applied comparative law has resulted in combinations and permutations of traditional doctrines which differ from country to country. In short, the eclectic principle has been used to adapt the law to the particular temper of a particular Muslim society today. This is a healthy process of social purpose and one which has given a new and a much deeper practical significance to the famous dictum of the Prophet: "Difference of opinion within my community is a sign of the bounty of Allāh."

# 3

# AUTHORITARIANISM AND LIBERALISM

References by the English judiciary to their Muslim counterparts, the *qāḍīs*, are understandably infrequent. When they do occur they are accordingly something of a curiosity. Thus, in *Metropolitan Properties Co. Ltd.* v. *Purdy*, 1940, Lord Justice Goddard, as he then was, remarked (in reference to the Courts [Emergency Powers] Act, 1939): "the court is really put very much in the position of a Cadi under the palm tree. There are no principles on which he is directed to act. He has to do the best he can in the circumstances, having no rules of law to guide him." Here is as good an expression as any of the popular notion of palm-tree jurisdiction, a quaint picture of the administration of justice in Islam as dependent upon the boundless discretion and arbitrary whim of the individual judge.

I propose to consider in this lecture what measure of freedom a Muslim judge or jurist in fact enjoys to determine the law, and to contrast in this respect the traditional attitude which dominated Islam from early medieval times to the present century with the new philosophy which is emerging today in contemporary Muslim States.

Islamic jurisprudence is a speculative essay to comprehend the precise terms of Allāh's law. In the preceding two lectures I have outlined the nature of this process of comprehension and observed the varying results that derived from it. The question to be asked now is what authority the resultant doctrine has commanded in practice both for the jurists whose task it was to expound the law and for the judges whose task it was to apply it. In the interpretation of the accepted texts of divine revelation or in the regulation of new cases, did the individual judge or jurist enjoy a personal freedom of decision, or was he required to follow some recognized authority? Because of the essentially tentative and speculative nature of Sharī'a law and because of the total involvement therein of the religious conscience, the tension between the notions of individual freedom and binding authority in this context is particularly acute.

To the general process of juristic endeavor to ascertain the terms of Sharī'a law is given the name *ijtihād*, the person thus engaged being known as a *mujtahid*. Naturally enough the scholars who were first in the field enjoyed full freedom of independent inquiry. But equally naturally, as time went by, the process of *ijtihād* became more circumscribed. This was not only because of the limitations imposed upon the process of *ijtihād* by developing jurisprudential theory itself—in its recognition that the raw material it had to work on was confined to the texts of the Qur'ān and the *sunna* and in its growing curtailment of the acceptable methods of juristic reasoning—but more particularly because of the practical circumstances surrounding the growth of the doctrine. The grouping of the scholars into schools, founded upon personal allegiance to outstanding jurists who had won the respect of their contemporaries, created a situation in which the disciples toed the party line and extolled the virtues and authority of their particular master almost to the point of canonization. This personality cult in fact developed despite the wishes of the leaders themselves, who had insisted upon the individual and fallible nature of their doctrines. The great jurist Shāfiʿī, for example, the father of Muslim jurisprudence himself, consistently repudiated the notion of a new school of law based upon passive acceptance of his teaching. And yet it was personal loyalty and allegiance to him which produced, after his death, the Shāfiʿī school of law.

Thus the doctrine of the early jurists came to be invested with an authority which they themselves had never claimed for it. Their written works became, in the language of jurisprudence, "the mother-books" of the school and were the subject of increasingly exhaustive commentaries by succeeding generations of disciples who faithfully preserved the basic substance and the format of the teachings of the old masters. The doctrine thus became settled and ratified, at least within each school, by the general consensus, and the belief gained ground, in the circles of jurists, that the process of *ijtihād* had run its full course. By the beginning of the tenth century it appeared that the labors of past generations of jurists had now brought the doctrine to maturity. Further *ijtihād* would be without purpose or profit. And at this point jurisprudence formally recognized that its creative force was spent. "The door of *ijtihād*," as the Arabic expression has it, "was closed." Future generations of jurists were denied the right of independent inquiry and were bound instead by the principle termed *taqlīd* to "follow" or "imitate" the doctrines of their predecessors. Those doctrines were now recorded in voluminous Arabic legal manuals which constituted for each school the comprehensive expression of Sharī'a law and enjoyed for the following ten centuries a paramount and almost exclusive authority as works of legal reference. No longer did the judge or jurist feel free to consider the text of the Qur'ān or the terms of the Prophet's precedents; not for them to reason by analogy or employ such equitable preference as had led to Umar's decision in the Donkey Case or the formulation of the celebrated Mālik's Rule. Now, as *muqallids*, or "followers," they must take the law from the authoritative manuals and not seek to go behind them. This applied whether the judge or jurist was sitting in the law school or in the court room in the mosque or even, though most improbably, under a palm tree.

Various theories have been advanced to explain this phenomenon of the closing of the door of *ijtihād* and the doctrine of *taqlīd*. It has been suggested, for example, that it arose from the political situation at the time of the Mongol invasions of Islamic territory. The Muslim jurists are supposed to have deliberately invested the legal manuals with a totalitarian and sacrosanct authority, so that the corpus of legal doctrine might, as it were, be enshrined and embalmed and so preserved from the corrupting influence of the vicissitudes of the times and the ravages of the barbarian hordes.

To my mind such theories are both fanciful and unnecessary. The fact is that the Muslim lawyers, like their counterparts the world over, were creatures of precedent, for whom the essential purpose of law was to stabilize the social order. Other historic legal systems, such as Roman law or the common law, have also known their periods, more or less prolonged, when the law remained static and its rules settled because, simply, they were in line with the temper of the society which they were designed to control. But when the social order has evolved and changed, then the settled law has been disturbed and its authority has crumbled. Islamic law has proved no more immune from this general process than any other legal system. It may have been that Islamic law remained settled and stable for an extremely protracted period. But this was essentially because Islamic society itself remained relatively static throughout this time. There was in fact no real social impetus to challenge the authority of the medieval legal manuals until the past few decades of the present century. But now, when Islamic society has come to accept different values and standards of behavior, the traditional doctrine has been challenged and the principle of *taqlīd* called more and more into question.

Certainly the legal tradition of ten centuries' standing was not discarded overnight. Although Muslim scholars and thinkers of the caliber of Muḥammad Abduh in Egypt at the turn of the present century and Iqbal in

India had openly rejected the doctrine of *taqlīd*, only in the past two decades has practical implementation been given to the thesis that the Muslim jurists and judges of today may determine the rules of Sharī'a law by independent interpretation of the basic texts of divine revelation.

I now propose to consider the results of this novel approach as it has emerged in the two areas of the Middle East and Pakistan and to show how it has brought about certain important changes in the traditional Sharī'a law of divorce.

Divorce under traditional Islamic law may be effected in one of three principal ways. First, by the mutual consent of the spouses, where the simple agreement of the parties dissolves the union without the necessity of any recourse to judicial proceedings. Second, by a judicial decree of divorce granting the petition of a wife who establishes that her husband is afflicted with a disease of mind or body, or is guilty of some matrimonial offence, such as cruelty, desertion, or failure to maintain, which makes married life intolerable for her. Last, but not least, by the unilateral termination of the marriage by the husband's exercising his power of what is known as *ṭalāq*, a process which is best termed, to distinguish it from the other forms of divorce, "repudiation" of his wife by the husband. According to the consensus of the traditional authorities, a husband's power of repudiation is arbitrary and absolute. He may exercise it at will, and his motive in doing so is not subject to scrutiny by the court or any other official body. His *ṭalāq* is entirely an extrajudicial process, unencumbered by any formalities. A repudiation repeated three times constitutes a final and irrevocable dissolution of the marriage. A single pronouncement of *ṭalāq*, on the other hand, is not final, for the husband may retract and revoke it at will during the period known as the wife's *'idda*, which lasts for some three months following the repudiation or, in cases where the wife is pregnant, until the birth of the child.

Without doubt it is the institution of *ṭalāq* which stands out in the whole range of the family law as occasioning the gravest prejudice to the status of Muslim women, and it is particularly in regard to this limb of the divorce laws that the doctrine of the traditional authorities has recently been superseded, in certain important respects, in the Arab countries of the Near East. Following the legal tradition of the Arab world it was the jurists rather than the judges who took the necessary initiative. It is their views which have found expression in the various codifications of Islamic law recently promulgated by governments in the Middle East—codes which have now supplanted the medieval legal manuals as the primary source of reference for the Sharī'a law which the courts are bound to apply.

A convenient focal point, for our purposes, is the Syrian Law of Personal Status, 1953. The preamble to the section of this Law which was concerned with divorce was forthright enough. The true purposes and incidents of divorce in Islam, it stated, had been misconstrued and perverted by the jurists of the past, whose doctrine had led to an appalling lack of security in married life. In this situation the proper policy was to "return to the origins of the law of divorce in Islam and adopt from outside (the four schools) provisions which will conduce to the public welfare." But after this clarion call of the preamble, the two major departures from the traditional law of *ṭalāq* come perhaps as something of an anticlimax.

First, the repudiation repeated three times, or the triple *ṭalāq*, was no longer to operate as an immediate and final rupture of the marital tie. It was to count as a single repudiation which could be revoked by the husband—with the aim, obviously, of allowing a cooling-off period and keeping open the door for reconciliation. The provision finds its juristic basis in the fact that there is no specific support for the traditional institution of the triple *ṭalāq* to be found in the Qur'ān or *sunna*; it was indeed argued that the triple *ṭalāq* was manifestly contrary to the spirit of the Qur'ānic texts which deal with divorce, and represented one of the perversions of the pure divine law referred to in the preamble.

Second, and more important, Article 117 of the Syrian Law enacts that where the court considers that a husband has repudiated his wife without reasonable cause and the wife has suffered material damage thereby, it may order the husband to pay the wife compensation. It is true that the legal remedies for the wife in these circumstances may seem not very extensive, since the limit of the compensation that the court may order is one year's maintenance and support. At the same time the provision constitutes something of a landmark in the development of Islamic Law. It represents the first real attempt, in thirteen centuries of legal tradition, to control the husband's power of repudiation. For the first time his motive in exercising his power was subject to scrutiny and the wife's position protected to some extent in the event of its abuse. In taking this independent line and contradicting the consensus of traditional authorities, the Syrian jurists claimed that they were returning to the original texts of divine revelation and giving proper implementation to general Qur'ānic injunctions which urge husbands both to exercise their right to repudiate "with consideration" and to make "a fair provision" for wives they have repudiated.

Four years after the Syrians had thus unlocked, and forced a foot inside, the door of *ijtihād*, it was heaved wide open by the Tunisians. The Tunisian Law of Personal Status, 1957, briefly declares: "Any divorce outside a court of law is devoid of legal effect." Where a husband desires to repudiate his wife he must appear before the court, which *must* issue a decree of divorce if the husband remains obdurate. But the court is empowered to decide, taking all the circumstances into account, whether the husband shall pay the wife compensation and, if so, what such compensation, without any limit being fixed by the law, shall be.

In support of the major innovation, the requirement that *ṭalāq* should now be effective only by judicial process, the Tunisian jurists claimed the authority of a verse of the Qur'ān which states: "Where discord arises between spouses, then appoint arbitrators." Since there could be no clearer indication of a state of discord between spouses than the desire of a husband to repudiate his wife, and since the courts were the most appropriate organ to fulfill the duty of arbitration enjoined in those circumstances by the Qur'ān, what more positive authority could there be for judicial intervention in all cases of *ṭalāq*? Of course the husband still retains the power to terminate the marriage unilaterally, subject to his readiness to pay compensation, but the final, knock-out blow to the patriarchal scheme of the traditional doctrine was still to come. A court, proclaims the Tunisian law, will grant a decree of divorce in three principal circumstances: first, where either party can establish a recognized ground for judicial dissolution of marriage, such as physical or mental disease or a matrimonial offence; second, in the case of the mutual agreement of the spouses to divorce; third, where *either party* insists upon a divorce, when the court will assess the proper compensation payable. In short, the Tunisian law now puts the wife in the matter of divorce on an exactly equal footing, in theory at any rate, with the husband. For this revolutionary step, again, it could be claimed that the Qur'ān itself provided the necessary authority, particularly in the verse (II, 228): "And women have rights similar to those that the men have over them." Perhaps there is no modern law of divorce today that enshrines more positively and more unequivocally than the Tunisian code the philosophy that divorce should be available when a marriage has in fact broken down.

From the attempts of the jurists in the Middle East to break free from the strictures of the doctrine of *taqlīd*, I turn now to the efforts of the judges in Pakistan. British influence in India prior to partition, and now carried over into Pakistan, has resulted in the unique phenomenon of Islamic law being administered essentially as a case-law system. It is to judicial precedent that the courts turn for authority rather than to the manuals of Sharī'a law. Of course the judicial precedents themselves long recognized the binding authority of the classical manuals. It may be that a judiciary whose mother tongue was not Arabic and who were particularly dedicated to the principle that their judgments should be based on "justice, equity and good conscience" were not dominated by the rigid doctrine of *taqlīd* to the same degree as their fellows in the Middle East. But, at the same time, the duty of the courts to apply the doctrine of the classical manuals in all fundamentals was firmly established.

In the leading case of *Aga Mahomed* v. *Koolsom Beebee*, 1897, the widow of a deceased Muslim claimed, in addition to her share of the inheritance, maintenance for one year from her former husband's estate. The court of first instance admitted her claim on the ground of a verse in the Qur'ān (II, 241) which reads: "Such of you as shall die and leave your wives ought to bequeath to them a year's maintenance." But the settled law as recorded in the authoritative legal manuals was that a widow had no such right of maintenance. The verse of the Qur'ān was regarded as repealed by the subsequent provision in the Qur'ān for the widow of a fixed share of the inheritance. For this reason the Privy Council, as the final court of appeal in this case, rejected the widow's claim to maintenance and observed: "Their Lordships . . . do not care to speculate on the mode in which the text quoted from the Koran . . . is to be reconciled with the law as laid down in [the authoritative manual of Ḥanafī law] the Hedaya. . . . But it would be wrong for the Court on a point of this kind to put their own construction on the

Koran in opposition to the express ruling of commentators of such great antiquity and high authority."

As long as the principle enshrined in Koolsom Beebee's Case prevailed, the only authority which could override the settled law of the classical manuals was the legislature itself. This has been done, as far as the law of divorce is concerned, on two major occasions. The first was the passing of the Dissolution of Muslim Marriages Act, 1939. Under traditional Ḥanafī law a Muslim wife has no right at all to petition the court for dissolution of her marriage on the ground of any matrimonial offence committed by the husband. She may petition the court to annul her marriage where the husband has proved totally incapable of consummating it, and she may petition the court for a declaration that she is a widow and that therefore her marriage is terminated. But she may only ask for such a declaration when her husband has disappeared and nothing has been heard of him for a period of ninety years counting from the date of his birth. Under the legislation of the Dissolution of Muslim Marriages Act, however, which was clearly modeled on the English Matrimonial Causes Acts, a Muslim wife was granted the right to petition for divorce on such standard grounds as cruelty, desertion, and failure to maintain.

The second piece of legislation was the Pakistani Muslim Family Laws Ordinance, 1961. This ordinance was the outcome of a protracted review of various aspects of the family law which had begun with the appointment of a commission of inquiry in 1955. As far as divorce was concerned, the commission had suggested that a husband should not be allowed to exercise his power of repudiation without the consent of the court, and that such consent should only be given where adequate provision could be made for the wife's future maintenance and support. But such was the opposition voiced by traditionalist elements against this proposal that it was sunk almost without trace before the legislature came to pass the ordinance. In effect, all that the ordinance achieves is the enforcement of a cooling-off period after the pronouncement of a *ṭalāq*, so that attempts may be made to reconcile the estranged couple. The ordinance sets up arbitration councils, consisting of a representative of each spouse and an independent chairman. A husband who repudiates his wife is obliged, under pain of fine or imprisonment, to inform the chairman of the arbitration council of this in writing. In no case will any *ṭalāq* be effective until a period of ninety days has elapsed since delivery of the written notice. During this period the function of the arbitration council is confined to attempts at reconciliation. It may be that the ordinance has thus abolished those forms of repudiation, such as the triple *ṭalāq*, which were final and irrevocable. But there is no question even of any compensation being payable by the husband, much less of a divorce being refused, so that the terms of the ordinance fall far short of the recommendations of the commission, and indeed of the Syrian and Tunisian Laws mentioned previously.

However, where the legislature feared to tread, the judges have stepped in, not, as yet, to restrict the husband's power of repudiation, but to even the balance between the spouses by giving the wife an almost parallel right to end the marriage unilaterally. To this end the courts have claimed the right to bypass the traditional authorities and ascertain the law by independent interpretation of the divine revelation.

The leading case in this regard, occurring in fact some two years before the legislation of the Family Laws Ordinance, is *Balquis Fatima* v. *Najm-ul-ikran Qureshi*, decided by the High Court of Lahore in 1959.

Balquis Fatima's marriage had been a marriage in name only and she had never lived with her husband. Eventually she petitioned for divorce under the Dissolution of Muslim Marriages Act on the ground that her husband had failed to maintain her. When this petition failed, it was argued that the High Court should nevertheless grant a divorce because, it was claimed, "a wife has a right, under Muslim law, to demand a divorce on returning to her husband any property or material benefit she may have received from him."

According to traditional Ḥanafī law a wife may obtain a divorce by providing the husband with some consideration, usually the dower money which she received from him on her marriage, for her release. This form of divorce is known as *khulʿ*. It is an extrajudicial method of divorce, not requiring any decree of the court. But since it is a divorce by mutual agreement, the free consent of the husband is essential for its validity. In Balquis Fatima's case, however, it was argued that the verse of the Qur'ān upon which the institution of *khulʿ* divorce is grounded allows the court, in certain circumstances, to enforce a *khulʿ* divorce upon the parties even without the husband's agreement thereto. The relevant text of the Qur'ān reads: "If you fear that the spouses cannot keep within the bounds set by Allāh, then there is no blame on them if the wife provides some consideration for her release." This verse, it was argued, must be addressed to the judge, who is asked to determine whether the spouses can keep within the bounds set by Allāh—in other words, whether the rift between the parties is so serious as to make married life intolerable. Now since a *khulʿ* divorce by agreement between the parties is effective whether their married life is tolerable or not, the only explanation of this reference to the judge must be that he has the power to end the marriage if in fact it has become intolerable to the wife. If he could not do so, if *khulʿ* could take place only with the agreement of the husband, any decision of the court that the parties could not keep within the bounds set by Allāh because their marriage had in fact broken down would be wholly pointless.

Accepting these arguments, the High Court ruled that a Muslim wife may demand a *khulʿ* divorce as of right—though not, the court was careful to add, "for every passing impulse," but only "where the judge apprehends that the limits of God will not be observed, that is . . . that a harmonious married state, as envisaged by Islam, will not be possible." The wife is obliged, of course, to restore to the husband what she received from him in consideration of marriage. Balquis Fatima had in fact received as her dower ornaments to the value of 2,500 rupees, and this sum was now paid by her to the husband as consideration for her release.

Although the decision in this case was clearly the result of the court's independent interpretation of the Qur'ān and constituted a radical departure from the traditional Ḥanafī law, it may be observed that the law of the Mālikī school, as applied, for example, in Morocco, Tunisia, or Nigeria, has always recognized that a *khulʿ* divorce may be effected upon the insistence of the wife despite the lack of any agreement by the husband. The Mālikī law here rests upon another verse of the Qur'ān which is closely allied to the verse concerning *khulʿ* and which reads: "If you fear discord between the spouses, then appoint an arbitrator from his family and one from hers." From this verse Mālikī law devised a special procedure in cases of matrimonial discord under which the two arbitrators investigated the cause of the rift. If attempts at reconciliation failed, the duty of the arbitrators was to decide which of the parties was primarily to blame for the breakdown of the marriage. If it appeared that the husband was primarily at fault, the arbitrators could order the husband to divorce his wife by *ṭalāq*, and, if he refused to do so, could pronounce the *ṭalāq* on his behalf. If, on the other hand, the main blame rested with the wife, the arbitrators were empowered to effect a *khulʿ* divorce, under which the wife would be obliged to return the dower in consideration of her release. This procedure could therefore be invoked by a wife to rid herself of an unwanted husband, however innocent and blameless his marital conduct may have been, provided she was prepared to pay for her freedom.

But to return to the position in Pakistan. After Balquis Fatima had assured herself of a niche in the annals of Islamic legal history—at least in the Indian subcontinent—there followed a series of decisions of the High Court which were based on the right of the courts to depart from the doctrines expounded in the classical legal manuals. The collective effect of these decisions was to dismember the doctrine of *taqlīd.* It was now left only for the remnants to be decently and finally interred. And this was duly done on the highest judicial authority of the Supreme Court in the case of *Khurshid Bibi* v. *Mohamed Amin*, 1967.

In this case the complaining wife, Khurshid Bibi, alleged ill-treatment by her husband. But her petition for divorce on the ground of cruelty failed, because the acts complained of, or at least those which were held proved by the court, did not amount to the necessary degree of legal cruelty. Nevertheless the Supreme Court gave its blessing to the previous decision of the High Court in Balquis Fatima's case. It was held that Khurshid Bibi could demand a divorce, as of right, provided she was prepared, as indeed she was, to return to the husband the dower she had received from him.

Such, then, is the extent to which, in the particular field of divorce law, the modern codifications of Islamic law in the Middle East and judicial decisions in Pakistan have broken the stranglehold of the doctrine of the medieval legal manuals. Although the use of independent reasoning is still very much the exception to the general rule, and although the great respect for the traditional authorities means, as a dictum in one Pakistani case has it, that they are "not lightly to be disturbed," there is a distinct trend today toward a greater freedom of independent enquiry to ascertain the terms of the religious law. Of course such enquiry may proceed only within strictly defined limits. Any proposed departure from the law of the classical authorities must be firmly grounded upon indications in the Qur'ān or the *sunna,* or at least not be contrary to any specific regulation thereof. Certainly it is a process of juristic reasoning far removed from the notion of the unlimited discretion and the arbitrary whim of the *qāḍī*, who sits, in the contemplation of the former Lord Chief Justice of England, under a palm tree, with "no principles on which he is directed to act" and "no rules of law to guide him."

# 4

# IDEALISM AND REALISM

In the three preceding lectures I have been principally concerned with the formulation and development of legal doctrine by the jurists of Islam. I now propose to focus attention more closely upon legal practice in Islam, upon the administration of law through the official tribunals of the Muslim state.

Appointment to the judicial office of *qāḍī* was far from being the ultimate aspiration of the traditional Muslim scholar-jurist, as the following remarkable incident, reported by a biographer of the jurists of Northwest Africa, may illustrate. In the year 788, Ibn Farūk, a jurist from the Mālikī center of Qayrawan, firmly refused the post of *qāḍī* offered to him by the local governor. However, the biographer recounts: "The governor forced him to take his seat in the mosque and ordered the litigants to address their pleas to him, while Ibn Farūk was weeping aloud and crying to them: 'Have mercy upon me, that Allāh may have mercy upon you.' As he refused to judge the case, the governor ordered that he be bound and taken up to the roof of the mosque and thrown over the edge if he persisted in his refusal. Ibn Farūk was taken up to the roof and asked: 'Will you do it?' 'No,' he replied. Whereupon the guards prepared to throw him off. But Ibn Farūk, perceiving now that they were in earnest, declared: 'I accept the office.' He was then installed in the mosque under guard. But when the first two litigants approached and stood before him, he looked at them and burst into tears . . . 'I implore you by Allāh,' he said, 'to free me from the burden of yourselves. Do not be the first of my ill-omens.' The two litigants took pity on him and departed." At this, we are told, the governor persisted no further but appointed another *qāḍī*.

Legal literature abounds with such expressions of distaste, on the part of the medieval jurists, for the office of judge. One Egyptian scholar, who went into hiding when he was sought for the office of *qāḍī*, remarks: "Am I to appear on the day of judgment, my Lord, as a *qāḍī*? Never! though I be severed by the shears." Another quotes an alleged statement of the Prophet: "He who is appointed *qāḍī* has his throat cut without a knife."[1]

These anecdotes illustrate the attitude of detached idealism which had come to dominate Muslim jurisprudence. During the early days of the formative period of the law, it is true, doctrine and practice were closely interrelated. The law grew out of the actual judicial

1. For the sources of these and similar anecdotes see my article "Doctrine and Practice in Islamic Law," *Bulletin of the School of Oriental and African Studies* (University of London) 18 (1956), pt. 2, pp. 211, 212.

decisions of the Prophet, his political successors like the Caliph Umar and his judgment in the celebrated "Case of the Donkey," and the early *qāḍīs*. The earliest scholars in the law schools also were often men of a practical outlook. Mālik's doctrine, for example, as recorded in the work known as *al-Muwaṭṭa'*, the first written compendium of Islamic law, rests firmly upon a recognition of the actual legal practice, or *'amal*, of Medinise society. So, too, the Ḥanafī scholar Abū Yūsuf was intimately connected with legal practice through his office of Chief Justice in the administration of the Caliph Hārun.

But with the jurisprudential debate which began toward the end of the eighth century and eventually produced the theory of the sources of law, came the notion of the Sharī'a as the comprehensive and preordained system of God's commands, a system of law having an existence independent of society, not growing out of society but imposed upon society from above. And the discovery of this pure law, it was felt, was a task best undertaken in isolation from practice. Muslim jurisprudence then became essentially an introspective science, concerned with the elaboration of the pure Sharī'a law *in abstracto* and content to leave the mundane matter of the enforcement of the doctrine it expounded to the officials of the State. This idealism of the medieval jurists, who adopted the role of spiritual advisers to the conscience of Islam rather than practical administrators of its affairs, created a decided rift between legal doctrine and legal practice and a clear division between the role of the jurist and the role of the judge. In Islam, therefore, there is a particularly significant tension between the legal ideal and the social reality; and I now address myself to the broad question of the extent to which the pure doctrine was translated into actual practice. How far does the reality of law in Islam conform to the ideal system of the Sharī'a as expounded by the jurists?

What must first be considered is the way in which the jurists themselves visualized Sharī'a law being administered. What scheme did the jurists propound, in terms of the constitution of courts and the rules of procedure and evidence they should follow, for the application of the substantive law to actual disputes? The doctrine recognizes only one organ for the administration of Sharī'a law — the court of a single *qāḍī*. It makes no provision for courts with a plurality of judges nor for any system of appeal. There is no jury system, the single *qāḍī* being the judge of both facts and law, and no formal provision for representation — both these institutions absent simply because the rigid system of procedure and evidence makes fact-finding an almost automatic process and advocacy wholly superfluous. Upon each fact in issue, whether it be initial, intermediate or ultimate, one party, whom we may call the plaintiff, will shoulder the burden of proof. To discharge this burden of proof, he must normally produce two witnesses to give oral testimony of the truth of his claim. The witnesses must be male, adult Muslims. The testimony of women is admitted in certain cases, though usually on the basis that two women are needed in the place of one man — a general characteristic of Islamic law being to rank the female at half the tariff of the male. Furthermore, to qualify as a witness a person must possess a quality of high moral integrity which is known as *ʿadāla*; that is to say, according to a generally accepted definition, he must not, at least, have been guilty of any single serious offence against law or morality or of the persistent commission of less serious offences. Finally, the two qualified witnesses must testify directly to their personal knowledge of the truth of the plaintiff's claim. Circumstantial evidence is normally rejected by Sharīʿa doctrine. When it is admitted, by way of exception, it must be so strong as to appear, to the external observer at any rate, well-nigh conclusive.

Thus, any extramarital sexual relationship amounts to the criminal offence of *zinā* under Sharīʿa law. But it is only the Mālikī school that regards this offence as proved by the birth of a child to a girl who has never been married. Again, the prosecution in a case of homicide might produce two qualified witnesses to testify that they heard the sounds of a violent struggle in a house, that they saw the accused emerge from the house with a blood-stained knife in his hand, and that the house was empty save for the body of the victim. Yet Sharīʿa doctrine forbids the judge to draw from this evidence the conclusion that the accused was the killer. Such evidence constitutes what is termed "suspicion." It may result in the conviction of the accused if it is supported by fifty confirmatory oaths taken by the relatives of the victim and swearing to the guilt of the accused. Alternatively, the acquittal of the accused in such circumstances may require fifty oaths of his innocence sworn by his relatives. But the evidence itself is never conclusive.

The basic requirement of two witnesses to discharge the burden of proof applies both to the prosecution in a criminal case and to the plaintiff in a civil suit, except that the latter, in regard to certain claims, may prove his case by producing one witness and himself swearing an oath as to the truth of his claim. Where the required proof is produced, judgment must be given in favor of the plaintiff. Where the plaintiff produces no real evidence, judgment will be given for the defendant. But where the plaintiff produces evidence which is substantial but yet does not fulfill the strict requirements—for example, if he has only one qualified witness, or witnesses whose integrity is in some doubt—the onus then passes to the defendant, who is offered the oath of denial. Properly sworn, such an oath will secure judgment in his favor; whereas, if he refuses to take it, judgment will be given for the plaintiff, provided, in some cases, the latter is prepared to swear to the truth of his contention.

The outstanding feature of this system of procedure and evidence is the way in which it deliberately restricts the scope of the individual judge's discretion in the matter of fact-finding. There is no test of the credibility of a witness on the facts to which he testifies, by cross-examination or any other means. The judge does not have to weigh the evidence of one side against that of the other and come to a decision on the balance of probabilities. In effect he has only two preliminary tasks to perform: to determine, first, which party carries the burden of proof and, second, whether the witnesses that are to be called are qualified, on grounds of integrity of character and so forth, to testify or not.

Once these two issues have been decided and the legal process set in motion, the judge merely presides to see that the process follows its prescribed course. The testimony is given, the oath is administered or refused, and the verdict follows automatically.

The system was, I think, a conscious attempt by the jurists who formulated it to absolve the judge as far as possible from any direct responsibility for a miscarriage of the divine law. Because the testimony of the witnesses or the oath was decisive and binding upon the judge, and because it was merely the duty of the judge to apply the law to the facts as thereby established, it was as though the responsibility for a wrong conclusion as to the facts lay with the parties themselves. The fear of a miscarriage of the law was a very real one for the Muslim scholars and was the principal reason for their declared aversion to judicial office. An English Chancery judge, referring to the difficulties which confront the judge when he is attempting to construe the intention of a testator from the words in his will, is alleged to have said: "I shudder to think that in the hereafter I shall have to meet those testators whose wishes on earth have been frustrated by my judgments." There awaited the Muslim *qāḍī* who misconstrued the religious law a much more serious situation in the world to come—namely, the wrath of the Lawgiver himself.

Clearly the Sharīʿa rules of evidence reflect the idealism of the Muslim jurists. The strict burden of proof imposed upon the plaintiff or prosecutor requires him to establish his claim to a high degree of certainty, on the principle that it is better for several actual offenders to escape liability than for one innocent person to suffer liability. This attitude finds what is perhaps its zenith in the rule that for proof of the offence of fornication, four qualified, male, adult, Muslim eyewitnesses of the carnal act itself are required. In practice, however, and particularly in the general field of criminal law, the rule of oral testimony places an unrealistic burden on the prosecution. It is questionable, at least, whether the premise that a witness of hitherto blameless character will most likely tell the truth in the particular case for which he is called is a sound one; but in any event criminal offences are not normally committed in the presence of two male adult witnesses of high moral probity. Where the prosecution fails to produce the requisite oral testimony, the defendant will secure his acquittal by swearing an oath of innocence. Certainly the swearing of a religious oath in the *qāḍī*'s court is not a matter lightly regarded in traditional Muslim society. And it is a well-established fact that many accused, whose guilt is reasonably certain but has not been established by the requisite legal proof, refuse to swear the oath of denial when it is offered to them. At the same time the use of the oath in this decisive way may perhaps appear to reflect a somewhat altruistic reliance upon the force of religious conviction. It supposes that considerations of physical liberty and well-being in this world will be subordinated to those of spiritual satisfaction in the world to come.

Finally (and it is here perhaps that the idealism of the doctrine is at its most evident), in cases of conflicting testimony where the *qāḍī* feels unable to come to a correct decision on the basis of the evidence offered, he is allowed to abstain from judgment. "If no positive indication appears to him," writes one jurist, "then let him abandon the case and refrain from judgment, there being doubt in his heart."[2]

It is essentially because of the idealistic scheme of procedure and evidence and the self-imposed limitations of the Sharī'a as a practical system of law that there have existed in Islam since early medieval times jurisdictions other than that of the *qāḍī*'s court. The *qāḍīs* had never formed an independent judiciary in the true sense of the term. Appointed by the political ruler and subject to dismissal by him, they exercised their judicial office as his delegates. And when, because of their allegiance to the idealistic Sharī'a doctrine, their administration of justice proved defective, the ruler simply appointed other delegates.

This extra-Sharī'a jurisdiction assumed a variety of forms. There was, for example, the summary jurisdiction in petty commercial affairs of the inspector of the marketplace; and of the chief of police in criminal cases. Another judicial officer was appointed solely to resolve cases which the *qāḍīs* failed to resolve because they could come to no proper decision on the basis of the evidence offered. But the most important of these alternative jurisdictions was that of the official known as the "Master of Complaints," or *Ṣāḥib al-Maẓālim*. He came to have an extensive jurisdiction in those spheres where the speedy and effective administration of justice was of particular concern to the political authority—especially in criminal cases and in matters of land law. In a

2. Ibid., p. 224.

sense the various subordinate judicial officers I have mentioned may all be subsumed under the collective description of *Maẓālim* jurisdiction. The common feature of the various forms of *Maẓālim* jurisdiction was the latitude of discretion they enjoyed in matters of procedure and evidence. Their duty was simply to resolve litigation in the most effective way and on the basis of the best evidence available. While the *qāḍīs* became identified as the servants of the Sharī'a law, the *Maẓālim* officials were regarded essentially as the representatives of the political ruler's law. The distinction came dangerously close to a dichotomy between religious and secular jurisdiction, particularly as the usual seat of the *qāḍī's* court was in, or close to, the mosque, while that of the *Maẓālim* officials would be within the official residence of government.

Throughout the various and far-flung territories of Islam there was, of course, no standard pattern of relationship between the Sharī'a and the *Maẓālim* jurisdictions. In some areas the Sharī'a courts were restricted to the field of family law, but in others they retained an almost comprehensive jurisdiction. It depended, largely, upon the outlook of the individual *qāḍīs*. Some fought hard to preserve their jurisdiction by adopting a more realistic approach towards the practical application of the law. Thus, for instance, a scholar who accepted judicial office in Northwest Africa in the tenth century remarks; "It is almost impossible in these days to find a witness whose character comes up to the standard ideally required. Now it is our duty to apply the law to the best of our ability—that is all that Allāh requires of us. We must therefore accept the evidence of men in whom the good exceeds the bad—otherwise the rights of all men, the strong and the weak, will be lost, and the law will count for nothing."[3] But even a limited realism of this sort was the exception to the general situation in which the *qāḍīs* adhered strictly to the doctrinaire system of Sharīʿa procedure, and as a consequence were forced to yield to the growing encroachment of *Maẓālim* jurisdiction.

Ultimately, the rift that had come to exist between the ideal scheme of Sharīʿa law as expounded by the jurists and the actual legal practice in Islam, was recognized and ratified by legal scholarship under the doctrine known as *siyāsa sharʿiyya*, or "government in accordance with the precepts of divine law." Writers on constitutional law, from the eleventh century onwards, assert that while the Sharīʿa doctrine embodies the ideal order of things for Islam, the overriding duty of the ruler is to protect the public interest; and in particular circumstances of time and place the public interest might necessitate deviations from the strict Sharīʿa doctrine. Thus, states one writer: "Were we simply to subject each suspect to the oath and then free him, in spite of our knowledge of his habitual criminal activities, saying: 'We cannot convict him without two upright witnesses,' that would be contrary to *siyāsa sharʿiyya*."[4]

From this basis the doctrine of *siyāsa* proceeds to recognize the validity, on grounds of public policy, of

3. Ibid.

4. See my article "The State and the Individual in Islamic Law," *International and Comparative Law Quarterly*, January 1957.

the various forms of *Maẓālim* jurisdiction. In effect, the political ruler is recognized as the fount of all judicial authority, with the power to set such bounds as he sees fit to the jurisdiction of his various tribunals, including the Sharī'a courts. Certainly, in the contemplation of the constitutional lawyers, the Sharī'a doctrine remained the eternal ideal, and the alternative jurisdictions merely temporary deviations along the road to that ultimate aspiration. The doctrine of *siyāsa*, too, was based upon the assumption that the ruler was ideally qualified for his position—in terms of religious piety and knowledge of God's purposes for society. But the final submission of idealism to practical necessity comes with the doctrine of the constitutional lawyers that civil obedience is due even to the ruler who is in no sense qualified in this way. Public policy is often referred to, by Western judges seeking to safeguard the liberties of the individual, as "an unruly horse." The Muslim scholars had given this horse its head, and it had bolted. To the power of the ruler exercised on grounds of the public interest there were no constitutional limits. In the last analysis the extent to which Sharī'a law was applied through the jurisdiction of the *qāḍī*'s court depended upon the de facto power and the conscience of the political authority.

Although the basic reason for the limitation of the *qāḍī*'s jurisdiction lay in the system of procedure and evidence by which he was bound, there were also certain areas of the substantive doctrine of the Sharī'a where the idealism of the jurists clashed with the practical circumstances of life. Perhaps the most obvious instance of this lies in the doctrine of *ribā*. Basically a prohibition of usury, the concept of *ribā* had been rigorously and systematically extended by the jurists to cover, and therefore preclude, any form of interest on a capital loan or investment. Furthermore, since the doctrine was coupled with the general prohibition on gambling transactions, there fell within its ambit all kinds of speculative transactions, the results of which, in terms of the material benefits accruing to the parties, could not be precisely forecast. The law had thus come to reject from its ideal scheme of things types of contracts and business dealings which were in practice the lifeblood of commerce and the economy.

Here, too, there are examples of *qāḍīs'* courts showing a more realistic attitude to the practical needs of life and refusing to be hidebound by the strict terms of Sharīʿa doctrine. This has been particularly true of the Mālikī courts in Northwest Africa—that area of Islam traditionally known as Jazīrat ul-Maghrib, or "The island of the west." Here, for instance, a widespread form of land-holding was based on an agricultural contract under which the landlord leased the land to a tenant in return for a rental consisting of a quota part of the produce of the land. Usually, this quota part of the produce was a fifth, from which the contract takes its name of *khamessa.* According to pure Sharīʿa law the contract of *khamessa* was a nullity on the ground that the rental was too uncertain; first, it consisted of foodstuffs which were subject to fluctuation in market price; second, the precise value of the portion of one-fifth depended on the quality of the harvest and was unknown at the time the contract was concluded. In the contemplation of the doctrinaire jurists, this contract was fraught with risk and speculation. If the normal rental for the land when paid in cash was $x$ dinars, the actual rental in a contract of *khamessa* might be $x+$ or $x-$ dinars, according to the quality of the harvest. Hence, whether the gain, as against the norm, accrued to landlord or tenant, it was a speculative profit and tantamount to *ribā*.

Nevertheless, the contract of *khamessa* was widely practiced as something of an economic necessity in a society which had little floating capital, and eventually the Mālikī *qāḍīs* themselves recognized the validity of the institution, on grounds of necessity, so that it became an integral part of the Sharī'a law as applied by their courts.

Such realism, however, was exceptional. The *qāḍīs'* courts as a whole considered themselves bound by the doctrine as expounded in the Sharī'a manuals; and because this doctrine proved insupportable in practice, jurisdiction in matters of general civil law, contracts and commercial transactions, was assumed by other tribunals. Whether these tribunals were customary courts, or courts of arbitration set up by the merchant community itself, or a branch of the ruler's *maẓālim* jurisdiction, they had an official status, alongside the courts of the *qāḍī*, as part of the system of legal administration.

During the latter part of the nineteenth century the dichotomy in Islamic legal practice became much more pronounced. The presence of Western European powers in the Near and Middle East had produced a rapid expansion of trade and the development of novel commercial techniques. And as the most realistic way to cater for this situation, the Muslim countries of the Near and Middle East promulgated codes of commercial law and procedure based on European models. A similar large-scale reception of European law took place in the field of criminal jurisdiction. Substantive Sharī'a doctrine had here lost touch with the temper of Middle Eastern society generally. It was not only that the severe punishments prescribed by the Sharī'a for certain offences – such as death by stoning for adultery or amputation of the hand for theft – were now regarded, to say the least, as antiquated; it was also the case that offences against the person – from physical assault to homicide – were placed by Sharī'a law in the category of private wrongs, or torts, rather than public wrongs, or crimes. In such cases the decision whether or not to prosecute rested with the victim or his relatives, and in the event of a conviction the victim or his relatives had the choice between the sanction of retaliation – subjecting the offender to precisely the same treatment as he had handed out to his victim – or exacting compensation for the offence in the form of blood money, or pardoning the offender altogether. The law here reflected the tribal notion of private justice and was no longer practical inasmuch as the traditionally tribal structure of Muslim society had now largely disintegrated. Hence, new criminal codes were promulgated in most Middle Eastern countries, the source from which they were derived reflecting the dominant European influence in the country concerned. In Egypt and Northwest Africa the codes were of French inspiration; in the Sudan, basically English law was adopted, while the Lybian code was based upon Italian law.

Thus Sharī'a law had been generally abandoned in the fields of commercial law, general civil law, and criminal law. To apply the new codes, a new system of courts was created; and though these might be regarded as the modern descendants of the *Maẓālim* jurisdictions of former times, the law and its administration in these spheres was now frankly and openly secular.

Family law, on the other hand, remained firmly within the jurisdiction of the Sharī'a courts. This did not mean, of course, that the courts continued to apply the substantive doctrines of the traditional authorities. As has been observed, the content of Sharī'a law has been profoundly modified in recent times, in a variety of ways, to conform to the changing standards and values of contemporary society. So, too, the rules of procedure and evidence by which the courts are bound have changed; and the rigid idealistic scheme of the traditional doctrine has been relaxed in many respects. Of particular interest and significance, perhaps, in this regard is the way in which the doctrine of *siyāsa* has been invoked to introduce changes in the law of evidence which a realist approach to the circumstances of modern society seemed to require. Under the principle of *siyāsa* that the political ruler has the power to confine the jurisdiction of his courts, the Sharī'a tribunals have been denied the competence to hear cases which do not fulfill certain evidential requirements.

By this means, for example, it was sought to enforce a system of official registration of marriages and divorces. Pure traditional Sharī'a law rejects any form of documentary evidence—on the ground, one supposes, that a forgery which would deceive the court was a very likely possibility in the circumstances and times when the doctrine was formulated. Under modern conditions, however, the traditional rule that a marriage or divorce could be proved only by the oral testimony of qualified witnesses led to much abuse and injustice in practice. Hence the Sharīʿa courts in Middle Eastern countries generally are now forbidden to entertain claims arising out of a marriage or divorce which cannot be proved by the registrar's official certificate. A marriage or divorce which is not registered is not invalid on that ground; but a party whose claim arises out of such a marriage or divorce will find no judicial relief forthcoming. For this case is now outside the competence of the courts, whose jurisdiction is confined to matters arising out of a marriage or divorce which has been duly registered.

In the same fashion, though perhaps somewhat more subtly, the sovereign's power of *siyāsa* was used to prevent the Sharīʿa Courts from deciding issues of paternity on the basis of certain traditional evidential presumptions. Traditional Ḥanafī law recognized a presumption that the gestation period could last for two years and that a woman could be pregnant for this time. According to the other schools the period of pregnancy could last even longer—five years in the Mālikī doctrine. The basic reason, perhaps, for such long periods was the same excessive caution which the jurists displayed in such rules as the necessity of four eye-witnesses to establish the offence of fornication, or the rule that a missing person cannot be presumed dead until a period of ninety years has elapsed from the date of his birth. In modern times, however, with authoritative medical opinion setting the period of gestation at a maximum of one year, the traditional Sharī'a law occa sioned manifest injustice. For example, a child born to a widow just short of two years after her husband's death would be presumed to be the legitimate child of the former husband and there entitled, *inter alia,* to inherit the lion's share of his estate. Upon those who sought to deny the claims of this dubious child would lie the almost impossible onus of proving that it was, in fact, illegitimate. Hence, to remedy this and other mischiefs, an Egyptian law of 1929 enacted that the courts were not to hear any disputed claim of legitimacy on behalf of a child born more than one year after the termination of the mother's marriage with the alleged father. For all practical purposes now, therefore, the recognized legal limit of a period of pregnancy was one year. The jurisdiction of the courts to determine questions of paternity was confined to cases in which the factual situation involved was not contrary to the notions of modern medical science concerning gestation. The authority of the traditional doctrine was not expressly or directly denied; it was simply that the courts had now no competence to determine cases which necessitated the recognition or rejection of that traditional doctrine.

The tension, then, between idealism and realism in Islamic law can be simply expressed in terms of the distinction between legal doctrine and legal practice. A realist approach to the question of the role of law in Muslim society has meant in the past, and means even more so today, that the idealism of the doctrine both in matters of substance and procedure, has perforce had to give way to the needs of State and society in practice. Certainly, traditional Sharīʿa doctrine remains for many the comprehensive and ideal system of life for the golden age of Islam, whether past or future. And even for its more outspoken critics it remains the focal point of legal thought, exercising a pervasive influence as the touchstone by which alternative doctrines and institutions are to be measured and assessed. But for all this, Sharīʿa doctrine, both in historical tradition and contemporary practice, forms only a part of the actual Islamic legal system.

# 5

# LAW AND MORALITY

The problem of law and morality was recently the subject of a lively debate among lawyers in Britain following the now famous decision of the House of Lords in *Shaw* v. *the Director of Public Prosecutions*, 1962. Mr. Shaw had compiled a booklet entitled "Ladies Directory," which listed the names and addresses of prostitutes and included nude photographs and brief indications of their particular sexual practices. Apart from being guilty of publishing an obscene article, Mr. Shaw was also convicted of the offence of conspiring to corrupt public morals. It was the formulation, by the English law lords, of this last offence that stimulated discussion of the fundamental question: Is it the function of the law to enforce the standards of conventional morality by punishing deviations therefrom, particularly in cases of sexual immorality in private which does not occasion harm or offense to other persons?[1]

1. See H. L. A. Hart, *Law, Liberty, and Morality* (London: Oxford University Press, 1963), pp. 6–12.

Islamic law embodies the principle of strict enforcement of sexual morality in the severe punishment it prescribes for the offence of *zinā*, or fornication. Under English law a sexual relationship outside marriage is not a legal offence unless it is aggravated by circumstances such as lack of consent, the young age of the girl, the blood relationship of the persons concerned, or unnatural behavior, which will amount to the criminal offences of rape, unlawful carnal knowledge, incest, bestiality, or sodomy. Islamic law, on the other hand, holds that any sexual relationship is a crime unless it is between husband and wife or was, in the old days, between a master and his slave concubine. At the same time, the liability of the parties to an act of *zinā* for punishment cannot, in practice, be dissociated from the rules relating to proof of the offence. This must be established by the eyewitness of four adult Muslims of established integrity of character. No doubt an act of sexual immorality committed in circumstances where such testimony is forthcoming would amount at least to the criminal offense of public indecency even under English law.

The manuals of Sharīʿa doctrine lay down many other standards of sexual morality. The duty of fasting in Ramadan, for example, involves abstention from sexual intercourse as well as from food and drink—a rule which has certain legal implications. A wife's claim to her dower, for example, or her child's status of legitimacy may depend upon whether the law presumes her marriage to have been consummated or not. In general terms, the law presumes that a marriage has been consummated when the husband and wife have been together in circumstances of privacy when there is no objection under Sharīʿa doctrine to sexual relations. Such an objection does exist during the fast of Ramadan, so that circumstances of privacy occurring then would not give rise to the legal presumption of consummation of a marriage. But these legal effects are incidental: the rule is essentially a moral one inasmuch as its infringement does not occasion legal punishment.

However, a person who does break the duty of the fast in this, or in any other way, ought to atone for his sin either by fasting for additional days or by performing some charitable act of almsgiving. There is, therefore, in Islamic society a positive coercion toward the observance of this rule. It does not represent merely a moral standard in the sense that this term would bear in a secular society, where infringement of the standard would entail, at most, the general disapproval of society at large and perhaps a twinge of the individual's conscience. The Muslim offender may not have put in jeopardy his physical liberty or integrity; but he has certainly put in peril his spiritual salvation. An offense against the Islamic religious ethic is an offense against the law of God as surely as any other offense for which the courts would mete out punishment. The Islamic Sharīʿa is, in our terminology, both a code of law and a code of morals. It is a comprehensive scheme of human behavior which derives from the one ultimate authority of the will of Allāh; so that the dividing line between law and morality is by no means so clearly drawn as it is in Western societies generally. This is why, for example, such importance and significance attaches to the pronouncements of Muslim jurists on current problems like contraceptive birth control. Still, Islam does observe the distinction, in the narrow field of sexual behavior, between the rule which is enforced by the law as applied by the courts and the rule which finds its sanction only at the Bar of eternity. And I turn now to the broader issue of law and morality in Sharī'a doctrine as a whole. How far does Muslim jurisprudence, both past and present, distinguish between behavior which is ethically desirable and that which is legally enforceable? Or how far does it insist that it is the duty of the courts to compel a person to behave as ideally he ought to behave?

In the primary material source of the Sharī'a, the Qur'ān, there is no clear or consistent distinction between the moral and the legal rule. As the formulation of the Islamic religious ethic, the Qur'ān is concerned with fundamentals – to distinguish right from wrong, good from bad, proper from improper. It does not usually proceed to the secondary stage of clothing these norms of behavior with legal consequences. In some cases, it is true, precise legal sanctions are imposed for an act or omission – such as the penalty of flogging for serious defamation or that of amputation of the hand for theft. But in general the Qur'ānic precepts merely indicate those standards of conduct which are acceptable or not acceptable to Allāh and express their results in terms of the Divine favor or disfavor. Thus wine drinking is a "sin" and an "abomination"; usury is "forbidden" (*ḥarām*); a wife's obedience to her husband is a "virtue"; those who wrongfully appropriate the property of orphans "shall burn in the flame."

The same predominantly ethical tone pervades the

expression of Sharīʿa doctrine by the earliest jurists of Islam. It must be remembered that these early scholars had been concerned, first and foremost, with the specifically ritual practices of Islam, such as the prayer, almsgiving and pilgrimage. Indeed, these topics always occupy pride of place in the later manuals of Sharīʿa doctrine, where the first chapters are devoted to them. Accordingly, when the early scholars proceeded further to consider that area of life which is made up by social relationships, they did so with essentially the same attitude as that with which they had considered the religious duties, and expressed themselves in the same language. The relevant act or omission was good or bad, right or wrong in the eyes of God. One of the most common expressions of a value judgment by the leading Medinise scholar of early times, Mālik b. Anas, is: "I see no harm in this." It was the relationship of the individual with Allāh which was the paramount concern of the early scholars, and Sharīʿa doctrine was initially formulated as the system of duties owed by man to his creator.

In theory, of course, the Sharīʿa has always been a totalitarian and comprehensive code of conduct covering every aspect of human life and regulating the individual's relations with God, with the state, with his neighbor, and with his own conscience on the same single basis of the dictates of the divine command. Thus, any human activity, any social institution in Islam has in the final analysis a religious significance. And it was, at root, this religious idealism which caused many jurists to stand aloof from legal practice and in particular to shun the office of judge. But by the time the Sharīʿa had achieved its maturity of expression in the medieval legal manuals there had emerged, in practice, a broad division between the religious duties that the individual owed to God and the social duties that he owed to his fellow men. Moreover, within the field of social relations there was an accepted distinction between standards that were legally enforceable through the courts and standards that were morally desirable though their observance was a matter left to the individual conscience.

This distinction is embodied in the scale of so-called "Sharīʿa values," which are attached by classical jurisprudence to the whole range of human behavior and activities. From the central category of acts classified as permissible (*mubāḥ*) — that is, acts which have no positive or negative value legally or morally — the scale extends on the positive side to the act which is "obligatory" (*wājib*). If the obligatory act is one of religious practice, such as the fast, the Sharīʿa courts will not enforce its observance. Although the Sharīʿa may prescribe forms of atonement for nonobservance of the duty, the real sanction for infringement lies in the divine displeasure. But if the obligatory act is a social duty, the courts will enforce its observance. A husband, for example, is bound to maintain and support his wife. His failure to do so may give rise to certain forms of legal constraint — such as his imprisonment or the forcible sale of his goods — or, alternatively, may give the wife the right to judicial dissolution of the marriage. At the extreme end of the negative side of the scale of values is the act which is prohibited (*ḥarām*). Some prohibited acts are regarded as purely personal matters of religious practice: for instance, the prohibition of eating the meat of pigs or of concluding a contract of sale at the time of the Friday prayer. The commission of such an act is not subject to any legal sanction, civil or criminal, but will be punished in the world to come. Most prohibited acts, however, come under the head of social duties and are either punishable at criminal law or null and void at civil law.

Between the two extremes of binding duty and absolute prohibition are two intermediate categories of acts. On the positive side of the scale is the act which is valued as "recommended" or "praiseworthy" (*mandūb*). This means an act where performance entails divine favor and omission divine disfavor. On the negative side of the scale is the "blameworthy" act (*makrūh*), where omission brings divine favor and commission divine disfavor. Here the dichotomy between law and religious morality is clear-cut. For neither to the "blameworthy" nor to the "praiseworthy" act attaches any legal sanction of punishment or reward, nullity or validity. It is, for instance, praiseworthy for a marriage guardian to act upon the wishes of his ward. He *ought* to do so. But if he does not do so and concludes a marriage contract on her behalf despite her opposition, the marriage will nonetheless be perfectly valid. So, too, certain types of divorce by repudiation are classified as particularly "blameworthy"—as, for instance, the so-called "triple repudiation," where the formula of *ṭalāq* repeated three times terminates the marriage finally and irrevocably. Nevertheless there is no doubt about the legal validity of this form of repudiation. There is, in fact, an alleged statement of the Prophet regarding divorce by repudiation which goes to the heart of this distinction between the legal and the moral rule as reflected in the scale of Sharī'a values. The Prophet's dictum states: "Of all things legally permissible, *ṭalāq* is the most blameworthy."

The distinction between the legally enforceable rule and the morally desirable rule is not, of course, the distinction between a rule which is observed in practice and one which is not. The real values and standards by which a society lives are not always and not merely those that the courts will enforce. There are often more powerful forces to compel the observance of standards of behavior than legal coercion. In traditional Islamic society a consciousness and an acceptance of the standards of religious morality was instilled into the population at large through the great influence wielded by men of religion in public and private office – through the religious teachers in educational establishments, through the imams of the mosques and the institution of the Friday sermon, nd through the *muftis*, or jurisconsults, whose advice given in a public or private capacity often indicated how the ethical principles of Islam were to be implemented in the practical circumstances of life. Moreover, a special public office existed in traditional Islam for the precise purpose of ensuring the observance of the rules of religious practice and morality. Known as the *Muḥtasib*, this official watchdog of public morality had a roving commission to fulfill the task described in the Qur'ān as "urging to the good and dissuading from the bad" (*al-amr bi'l-ma'rūf wa'l-nahy 'an al-munkar*), and had limited powers of summary punishment of offenders. On the broadest view of Islamic society, therefore, law and religious morality are often inextricably merged into a general philosophy of life; there is in fact coercion to observe the moral as well as the legal standard. But I am here principally concerned with the narrower issue of the role played by the Sharī'a courts in the implementation of Islamic standards of behavior. And for these courts there is a definite distinction between the rule that is legally enforceable and that which is morally desirable.

The different schools of Sharī'a law do not always speak with one voice on particular issues which fall within the general problem of the relationship between law and morality. One such issue of importance is the question of the extent to which the law should concern itself with the intent or motive underlying the outward act.

The schools are unanimous on such fundamentals as the principle that a guilty mind is a necessary ingredient of a criminal offense, so that a person is not liable for punishment unless he intended to commit the guilty act. In cases of civil injury, on the other hand, liability may be incurred for damage caused accidentally and without intent; for here the purpose of the law is not to punish the person who causes the damage but to compensate the person who suffers loss. So, too, there is general agreement that a legal right cannot be used solely for the purpose of causing injury to an innocent party. If, for instance, a husband who knows he is at the point of death exercises his right of unilateral repudiation against his wife with the intention of depriving her of her right of inheritance in his estate, his immoral purpose will vitiate his act to the extent that it will not have the legal effect of so depriving the wife of her right of inheritance.

Beyond these basic issues, however, the schools have two distinct approaches. One approach is that the legal effect of an act or transaction must depend upon the motive or intent which inspired it. This is the moralist attitude, of which perhaps the Ḥanbalīs are the most consistent advocates. The other approach is that it is not for the law to attempt to burrow inside the mind of the parties; it must accept and regulate their actions at their face value. This is the legally formalist attitude, which is a general characteristic of Ḥanafī law.

One example of this divergence between the two schools concerns the contract of marriage. Notwithstanding the facility of divorce, all the Sunnī schools are agreed that a contract of marriage is, in essence, an agreement to a lifelong union, and that therefore a purported marriage expressly contracted for a limited period of time is no marriage at all and a nullity in law. Under Ḥanbalī law a purported marriage contract is equally a nullity if, despite the absence of any express stipulation of a time limit, there is evidence that the parties in fact intended the union to be temporary. Under Ḥanafī law, however, evidence of the parties' inner intent is irrelevant. If the external and formal contract, oral or written, is in conformity with the legal requirements, the marriage is valid. The Ḥanafīs content themselves with the statement that any improper intent the parties may have is a matter "between themselves and Allāh."

Similarly, in the law of bequests, all schools are agreed that a bequest openly and expressly made for an illegal purpose, such as the building of a distillery or a brothel, is completely null and void. But the Ḥanbalīs go further and also declare to be void a bequest inspired by an improper motive—as, for example, where the testator bequeathes a sum of money to Mr. X in gratitude for having kept him supplied with liquor, or to Miss X in recognition of her services as his mistress. In Ḥanafī law the testator's inner intention to reward the legatees for their illegal conduct would not vitiate either of these bequests, which would be valid and effective.

But the distinction between Ḥanafī formalism and Ḥanbalī moralism is perhaps most evident in the matter of the so-called legal stratagems or devices, termed *ḥiyal*. These devices are not legal fictions of the type known to the history of the English common law, where the law assumed the existence of a fictitious situation to serve as the procedural basis for the trial of a given issue, say the title to freehold land. Nor are they merely instances of strict adherence to the letter of the law, of avoiding a liability on grounds of a legal technicality or by finding a loophole in the law. Nor, again, are the *ḥiyal* cases of the kind of practice, particularly familiar to Western societies today in the realm of tax law, where judicious management of his affairs may place a person outside the ambit of the particular regulations he finds oppressive. The Islamic *ḥiyal* are simply legal trickery, of no great ingenuity, with the blatant purpose of circumventing an established rule of the substantive law, as a few examples will serve to show.

A basic trick to avoid the rule that prohibited any form of interest on a capital loan was the routine of a double sale. Assuming that a moneylender and a borrower have agreed on a loan of $1,000 for one year at a 50 percent rate of interest, they will veil this real transaction behind the cloak of two ostensibly separate and valid contracts of sale. In the first contract the moneylender sells to the borrower some object for a price of $1,500 payable in one year's time – such a sale with payment deferred being perfectly valid in Sharī'a law. In the second and immediately ensuing contract, the borrower sells back to the moneylender the very same object for a price of $1,000 payable at once in cash. As a result of these two transactions the object of the two sales is back where it started, with the moneylender; the borrower has acquired $1,000 in cash and is under an enforceable obligation to pay the moneylender $1,500 in one year's time.

One of the most popular ways of tying up property in traditional Islam was by a settlement under the *waqf* system. The essence of a *waqf* lies in the relinquishment by the founder of his ownership of the property which is the subject of the settlement. The property henceforth belongs in perpetuity only to Allāh and therefore cannot be transferred by any form of alienation. This in itself is deemed to be an act of piety and religious merit on the part of the founder. The income from the *waqf* property will be enjoyed by the beneficiaries nominated by the founder in whatever manner he prescribes. The institution of *waqf* was therefore often used to establish a family settlement, the income being enjoyed by the founder's children or other relatives, generation after generation.

Apart from the acquisition of religious merit, the

appeal of such a form of settlement often lay in the fact that it enabled the founder to avoid the devolution of his property to his legal heirs in accordance with the rules of inheritance. By making a *waqf* of his property the founder could preserve his estate intact and avoid its fragmentation through division among the legal heirs; he could also exclude entirely from enjoyment of his property some of his legal heirs if he so chose, and could generally apportion the benefits of the property's income among his surviving family in a manner more acceptable to himself than the results of the rules of inheritance. An owner of property who acted in this way could hardly be accused of legal trickery to avoid the laws of succession; he was simply availing himself of facilities offered by the law for the disposition of his estate. But an owner who wished so to act would often want to retain the use or income of the *waqf* property for himself during his lifetime. The majority opinion of Sunnī law was that he could not do this; but there was a singularly obvious stratagem, or *ḥīla*, available to remove this obstacle. The founder simply nominated as the first and exclusive beneficiary of his *waqf* "the first-born son of Zaid b. Umar" or any other description which fitted only himself. It is difficult to imagine a more naïve stratagem than this; but it is recorded in the authorities as one of the *ḥiyal* by which a founder might in fact reserve for himself the income of his *waqf* property during his lifetime.

I take my final example of Islamic legal trickery from the field of family law. A husband who has divorced his wife by repudiation three times, whether on the same or separate occasions, is not allowed to remarry her. A bar to marriage arises between a couple so divorced which is only removed if, after the former wife's marriage to someone else and the consummation of the marriage, that marriage is terminated by due process of law. Such an intervening marriage on the part of the former wife is said to "make her lawful" again to the former husband who had repudiated her three times. It was not apparently an uncommon occurrence for husbands who had hastily pronounced a threefold repudiation of their wives to recant and wish to remarry them, without of course having to wait unduly long for, or suffer the indignity of, the wife's being first married to someone else. Hence there arose in practice the device known as *taḥlīl*, or "the process of making the wife lawful" again to her former husband by a sham intervening marriage. Those who offered their services for this purpose were known as *muḥallils*, or "those who make the divorced wife lawful to her former husband." They were usually eunuchs or boys below the age of puberty, who divorced by repudiation the woman they had ostensibly married as soon as the contract of marriage was concluded. These temporary marriages of convenience were recognized by the law as an effective stratagem to remove the bar to remarriage existing between a divorced couple.

Such, then, is the nature of the Islamic *ḥiyal*. It does not, I think, require more than a minimal sense of moral purpose to refuse to countenance the sham façade of legalism behind which the parties lurk to effect their illegal purpose. And the Ḥanbalī school, along with the Mālikīs, condemned the *ḥiyal* in no uncertain terms. But Ḥanafī law, and Shāfiʿī law, taking the activities of the parties at their face value and not inquiring further into the intention behind the overt act, accepted the *ḥiyal* as legally effective. It may be that the *ḥiyal* effected a socially desirable purpose. But to countenance them on this ground was to deny the fundamental principle of Muslim jurisprudence that the ends or purposes which law should serve were a matter for decision by Allāh alone. In any event, to suggest that the Sharī'a courts should in this way connive at a manifest illegality was to make a mockery of their role as guardians of the standards of Sharī'a law.

Legal practice in the Muslim world today has in one sense brought about a more clear-cut dichotomy than hitherto between the fields of law and religious morality. Secularization of the criminal and commercial law, by the adoption of Western codes and a system of secular courts to apply them in place of the Sharī'a law previously administered by the *qāḍīs'* tribunals, has meant, for example, that the drinking of alcohol and extramarital sex relations have generally ceased to be criminal offences, and that the ban on *ribā*, or the taking of interest on loans, under the civil law has been lifted. In many respects, of course, these standards continue to have a very real influence in Muslim society; and, indeed, there still are, today, officials charged with the task of ensuring that the moral standards of behavior are observed in public. Law, it is often said, reflects the soul of a society; but it is particularly true of Muslim society that the reflection does not provide a complete picture. Even so, these standards of behavior fall today strictly outside the province of the law as applied by the courts.

On the other hand, recent developments in the field of family law in the Middle East have produced a much closer synthesis of law and morality, in the sense that standards of behavior which were regarded by the traditional authorities as imposing only a moral obligation upon the individual conscience have now been transformed into positive legal requirements.

This is particularly evident in the reforms which have lately taken place in the matter of divorce by repudiation, (*ṭalāq*), and which, in general, seek to implement the ethical standard embodied in the alleged statement of the Prophet: "Of all things legally permissible, *ṭalāq* is the most blameworthy." The so-called triple repudiation, where the husband repeats the pronouncement of *ṭalāq* three times on the same occasion, was particularly blameworthy inasmuch as it terminated the marriage at once and finally, and afforded no opportunity for reconciliation. In most Middle Eastern countries today this form of repudiation does not have the legal effect it had under the traditional law. It counts as a single and therefore revocable divorce. The Syrian and Tunisian Laws of Personal Status, promulgated in 1953 and 1957 respectively, contain more extreme examples of the transformation of a moral standard into a legal duty in their provisions relating to the payment of compensation by a husband to a wife he has repudiated without just cause. For these provisions represent the enforcement by the courts of the Qur'ānic injunctions which urge husbands not to abuse their power of *ṭalāq*—injunctions which traditional jurisprudence had consistently regarded as binding only upon the husband's conscience.

Essentially the same approach has brought about restrictions upon the practice of polygamy. The Qur'ānic verse which permits a husband to be married to four women concurrently contains an injunction that co-wives should be treated with impartiality. To this injunction traditional Sharī'a doctrine gives a limited legal recognition in the rule that a wife in desertion might successfully defend her husband's suit for restitution of conjugal rights, and still retain her right to maintenance and support, if she could establish the lack of such impartial treatment. Mālikī law goes further and holds that the lack of impartial treatment might amount to such legal injury as would give the wife a good ground for the judicial dissolution of her marriage. But apart from these comparatively minor legal qualifications, the only real restriction upon polygamy lay in the husband's conscience or in his pocket. The jurists were content to leave the sanction for infringement of the rule of impartial treatment to the afterlife. As an alleged dictum of the Prophet has it: "He who favors one wife to the detriment of another will appear on the day of judgment with half of his body deformed."

Modern codes of personal law in the Middle East, however, have placed an altogether novel emphasis upon the Qur'ānic injunction as constituting a strict legal obligation binding upon the husband and a condition upon which the right of polygamy depends. Thus, under the Iraqi Law of 1959 a polygamous marriage requires the permission of the court, and the court is given a discretion to refuse permission "if any failure of equal treatment between co-wives is feared." The

Tunisian Law of 1957 pursues this notion to its extreme limit. It is evident from the Qur'ān, it argues, that equal treatment of co-wives is a legal condition of the right of polygamy. It is equally evident that in the circumstances of present-day society such equality of treatment, to the mutual satisfaction of the spouses, is in practice impossible. And with the failure of the condition the right dependent upon it must also lapse. On this ground the law tersely declares: "Polygamy is prohibited."

A final example of the legal enforcement in modern times of what was considered by traditional doctrine to be a moral obligation occurs in the law of succession at death. Under the Sharī'a rules of inheritance a son of the deceased completely excludes from inheritance any grandchild of the deceased, and in particular orphaned grandchildren whose own parent died before their grandfather. In Egypt, Syria, Tunisia, and Morocco this was considered to be unjust to the orphaned grandchildren, and provision was made for them by the so-called rule of "obligatory bequests." Under this rule such orphaned grandchildren take as a compulsory bequest from the estate of their grandfather an amount equivalent to the share of inheritance their own parent would have received, had he or she survived, within the maximum limit of one-third of the whole estate. This novel rule finds its juristic basis in the Qur'ānic "verse of bequests," which urges people to make bequests in favor of close relatives. Traditionally this verse was regarded as repealed by the subsequent rules of inheritance, or, at best, as indicating a moral obligation to provide, by way of bequest, for relatives in need who were not legal heirs. The verse is now construed as imposing a legal duty to so provide for near relatives in need. It is assumed that orphaned grandchildren will always fall within this category. And where the deceased has failed in his duty, the court will fulfill it for him by ordering a bequest to take effect in favor of the grandchildren and to take priority over any other bequests the deceased may have made.

It is evident, I think, from these few examples that in the domain of contemporary family law Islam is witnessing a resurgence of legal moralism. The courts applying Sharīʿa law today, in deciding whether a divorce is "for just cause," or whether a proposed polygamous union is without prejudice to the wife's right of equal treatment, or in making a bequest on behalf of a deceased who has failed in his personal duty to do so, are enforcing ethical standards which are at the root of Sharīʿa doctrine but which have long been ignored by the practice of the Sharīʿa courts. Under the terms of recent modernist legislation in the Middle East the courts are often bound to act, as the English judges in Shaw's case thought it proper for the English courts to act, in the capacity of "general censor and guardian of the public morals."

# 6

# STABILITY AND CHANGE

With the one exception of the particular topic of law and morality, the conflicts and tensions which have been the subject of the preceding lectures are all subsidiary and interrelated aspects of the supreme tension which faces contemporary Muslim jurisprudence—namely, that of stability and change in the law. Divine revelation, unity of doctrine deriving from a universal consensus, authoritarianism in the form of the doctrine of *taqlīd* and idealism, which sees Sharīʿa doctrine as the eternally valid scheme of life, are all factors which together make for a rigid stability of the law. On the other hand, human reason in law, the resultant diversity of doctrine, the liberalism which renounces the sacrosanct nature of past doctrine and permits independent enquiry, and a realist approach to the facts of life are all elements conducive to change and variation in the law. I have indicated in the previous lectures how contemporary Muslim jurisprudence tends to emphasize the latter group of concepts rather than the former in order to meet the manifest need of adapting the law to the new circumstances of modern life. My purpose in this concluding lecture is to consider in general terms the phenomenon of recent changes in the Islamic legal system and the significance of this in terms of developing jurisprudential thought. In this way the threads of the previous tensions and conflicts I have discussed will be drawn together.

Changes in the substance of Sharīʿa family law as applied by the courts in the past few decades have been of profound social significance. The status of women has been immeasurably improved – for example, by freeing them from the institution of a compulsory marriage concluded by their guardians, by safeguarding their position during marriage by allowing them to stipulate special terms or conditions in the marriage contract which will be enforceable against the husband, by granting them the right to petition for divorce where the husband is guilty of some matrimonial offence, and by restricting the husband's rights of polygamy and unilateral repudiation. But the advancement of Muslim women toward the goal of equality between the sexes, desirable an end though it may be in itself, is merely part of a much more fundamental evolution of Muslim society.

Traditional Islamic society rested upon the agnatic tribal group, the extended family of male relatives who traced their descent through male links from a common ancestor. Contemporary Islam has witnessed a progressive decay of tribal solidarity and a breakdown of tribal ties and organization. In many areas and communities the basic unit of society is the more immediate family group composed of parents and their lineal descendants. And within this group the female has naturally acquired a more elevated status and a more responsible role.

Modern developments in the law have reflected this new concept of family ties and responsibilities in a variety of ways, but particularly, perhaps, through some significant changes in the law of succession at death. Under the traditional Sunnī law of inheritance, a daughter or granddaughter who is the sole surviving issue of the deceased is restricted to a share of one-half of the inheritance, and the residue of the estate will go to the brothers or more distant male agnate relatives of the praepositus. Today, however, under Iraqi law any female descendant of the deceased will totally exclude any collateral male agnate, as will a daughter or agnatic granddaughter under Tunisian law. And there is one other important reform in the law of bequests which deserves notice in this context. According to the consensus of traditional Sunnī authorities, a person may not validly make any bequest in favor of a relative who is entitled under the rules of inheritance to take a share in the estate as a legal heir. In the Sudan, Egypt, and Iraq, however, this rule has now been abandoned, and a testator has freedom to make bequests in favor of whomsoever he wishes within the limit of one-third of the net estate.

This reform was perhaps primarily designed to allow testators to distinguish between one legal heir and another by making additional provision for those thought to be particularly in need. But at the same time a testator may now increase considerably the share of his estate to which relatives of the immediate family might otherwise be restricted. The rule thus might be used for the benefit of his wife or his daughter or his granddaughter, in order to reduce the share of the total estate to be claimed as inheritance by some distant agnatic relative. In other words, this permissive rule may achieve results similar to those aimed at by the mandatory rules of inheritance I have just referred to—namely, the strengthening of the claims to succession of the more immediate family circle as against those of the tribal heirs.

Equally as radical as these substantive reforms have been the changes which have taken place in recent years in the form in which Sharīʿa law is applied through the courts. Throughout the Middle East generally Sharīʿa family law is now expressed in the form of modern codes, and it is only in the absence of a specific relevant provision of the code, or where difficulties of interpretation arise, that recourse is had to the traditionally authoritative legal manuals. In most countries too, the court system has been, or is being, reorganized, to include, for instance, the provision of appellate jurisdictions. In Egypt and Tunisia the Sharīʿa courts, as a separate entity, have been abolished, and Sharīʿa law is now administered through a unified system of national courts. Although the *qāḍīs* were absorbed into the staff of the national courts, the new system must eventually result in a deep change of character in the judges who apply Sharīʿa law. Indeed, one of the objects behind the codification of Sharīʿa law was to make its substance more accessible to a judiciary which was not trained in the particular skills and expertise required to ascertain the law from the labyrinth of the Arabic legal manuals.

Behind and in support of these developments lies an evolving system of legal education in Sharī'a law, which is now being studied, through the medium of modern textbooks and so forth, as an integral part of a general law curriculum. The trend behind all this is clear enough; it is that Sharī'a law, in the field of family relations — to which it is now generally restricted — should conform, in its expression in codes, in the procedures and techniques of the courts through which it is applied, and in the methods of legal education, to the standards which obtain in the general law — that is to say the civil, commercial, and criminal laws which were originally borrowed from European sources and which have now been absorbed into the Muslim way of life. In this way the dichotomy that has existed between the Sharī'a family law on the one hand and the general law on the other will be bridged, and Sharī'a law will become an integral part of the national legal system. The result, of course, will be that Sharī'a law will become externally divorced from religion, not of course in the sense that it will cease to have a religious significance, but in the sense that it will lose its traditionally close and exclusive association with religious personages and institutions and become instead the province of the professional lawyer.

Such a development is not, of course, without its fierce critics. Perhaps I may refer here briefly to a personal experience which is pertinent to this point. I was privileged to be concerned in the establishment, at Ahmadu Bello University in the Northern Provinces of Nigeria, in 1966, of a Center of Islamic Legal Studies. In general terms, this center was designed, with the approval of the Chief *Qāḍī* (or *alkali* in Hausa) and the leading Muslim jurists and judges of the Sharī'a Court of Appeal, to set Islamic legal studies on a modern footing. But when the question of the geographical site of the center was being considered, the view was put forward that it should be part of the College of Arabic and Islamic (religious) studies—which lay at a distance of about one hundred miles from the Law School. It was only after some debate that it was decided that the proper site for the center was within the Law School.

However, these recent changes in the substance and form of Sharī'a law are but the external manifestations of a fundamental change in the very heart of Islamic legal philosophy. As opposed to Turkey, which in the 1920s abandoned the Sharī'a law altogether in favor of the Swiss civil code, the other Muslim countries of the Middle East have followed a path of legal reform by evolution rather than by revolution. The process of adapting the Sharī'a to the circumstances of modern life was at first a tentative one. The doctrine of *siyāsa*, invoked by the ruling authorities to restrict the competence of the Sharī'a courts by procedural devices or to order them to apply some variant doctrine from another school, did not seriously shake the stability of Sharī'a doctrine. But when the reformers passed on to challenge openly the traditional doctrine and to claim the right to reinterpret the divine revelation in the light of current social needs, an altogether new situation developed. Change in the law was now accepted as legitimate and desirable and not merely as a necessary deviation from an immutable ideal standard.

From this progression of the reform movement there is now emerging a distinctly novel attitude toward the root question of the role and nature of the divine command in law. The attitude of classical and traditional jurisprudence to this question rested upon two fundamental and unassailable propositions; first, that the divine revelation prescribed rules and standards that were valid in all conditions and for all time; second, that the divine revelation answered, directly or indirectly, every legal problem. In short the divine command was comprehensive and eternally valid. Neither of these propositions remains unqualified by contemporary Muslim legal philosophy.

On the one hand there is perceptible support for the idea that the divine command itself visualizes a changing social order. This attitude was fairly openly adopted by President Habib Bu Ruqayba of Tunisia in his broadcast address to introduce the new *Law of Personal Status* which came into force in 1957. This law, as I have already observed, prohibited polygamy, on the juristic basis, according to the preamble to the code itself, that present-day circumstances made it impossible for the Qur'ānic condition of equal treatment of co-wives to be properly fulfilled. In his address, however, the president referred to the fact that "ideas which were valid in the past today offend the human spirit—such as polygamy . . . ," and went on to state that "polygamy has become inadmissible in the twentieth century and inconceivable by any right-minded person." Since he also declared that the law had "not contravened any Islamic principle," it must follow that in his view the Qur'ānic permission of polygamy was not intended to be operative in all places at all times.

This attitude toward the divine revelation is comparatively easy to maintain in relation to rules and institutions of the Qur'ān which are of a permissive nature—like polygamy or slavery. Such matters fall within the ambit of the principle of *ibāḥa*, or the "tolerance" of the Lawgiver; and there has always been considerable support for the view that something which is permitted or tolerated by the divine revelation may be restricted or even prohibited by the political authority if the general public interest so requires. This, it is said, is the particular significance of the Qur'ānic command "to obey Allāh, his apostle, and those at the head of affairs." But the case is different with those precepts of the Qur'ān which are of a mandatory nature—such as the specific command to cut off the hand of the thief or to flog those guilty of fornication. The fact that these Qur'ānic laws have in many places long been a dead letter has never been justified, to my knowledge, on the ground that they were not intended to be operative for all time. If such a view exists, it has remained subconscious and unexpressed. It has been argued in Pakistan, I know, that the application of the severe Qur'ānic penalties for extramarital sex relations would be most unjust in the circumstances of modern life, on the broad ground that the strong temptation and incitement toward such activities that is induced today through literature, the cinema, and television makes the offence inevitable. But this is an argument of temporary concession occasioned by the supposed degeneration of modern society; it does not question in any way the eternal validity of the Qur'ānic penalties as part of the ideal scheme of things. There is, in fact, in Pakistan today a movement to reassert this basic proposition. A. R. Cornelius, until very recently Chief Justice of the Supreme Court of Pakistan, has expressed himself in favor of the reintroduction of amputation of the hand as the ultimate penalty for theft; and this is being seriously considered, I am informed, by those scholars and jurists who are currently engaged upon a restatement of Islamic Law as it is in future to be applied in Pakistan.

As to the classical doctrine of the comprehensive nature of the divine revelation and its derivative principle that any legal rule must stem from divine revelation either directly, by being based upon a text of the Qur'ān or *sunna*, or indirectly by strict analogical deduction therefrom, this is gradually giving way to the attitude that the human intellect is free to determine a legal rule unless the relevant matter has been expressly regulated by the divine revelation. Therefore, outside the standards specifically laid down in the Qur'ān or the *sunna*, no further justification for a legal rule is required than the broad ground of its social value and desirability. Both the legislature and the judiciary in Pakistan have unequivocally endorsed this view.

The Muslim Family Laws Ordinance, 1961, introduced into the system of inheritance the rule of representational succession by orphaned grandchildren of the deceased. Any such grandchild now steps into the shoes of his or her predeceased parent and is entitled to inherit from the grandfather's estate what the predeceased parent would have inherited had he or she survived. It will be recalled that when the Egyptian reformers in 1946 had sought to achieve the same social purpose of making some provision for orphaned grandchildren in the law of succession, they had found it necessary to proceed indirectly through the rule of obligatory bequests, because it was only for such a rule that the specific authority of the divine revelation could be claimed—namely the Qur'ānic "verse of bequests." But the Pakistani reformers felt able to introduce the representational rule directly into the system of inheritance simply because it was not contrary to any specific rule of the Qur'ān or the *sunna.*

The same doctrine was voiced by the judges of the High Court of Lahore in *Khurshid Jan* v. *Fazal Dad,* 1964. The legal issue involved in Khurshid Jan's case was a relatively minor point concerning dissolution of marriage. Under traditional Ḥanafī law a minor girl may be validly contracted in marriage by her guardian. On attaining puberty, however, the girl has the right to repudiate the marriage provided it has not been consummated. In this case a wife purported to exercise this so-called "option of puberty," and, following the normal procedure, filed a petition for a decree of divorce on this ground. However, after filing the petition and before any decree had issued, the wife cohabited with the husband for a period of some fifteen days. The question that arose, therefore, was whether this cohabitation nullified her option to repudiate the marriage. The court of first instance decided that it did not, on the ground that it was the wife's declaration of repudiation of the marriage, as contained in her petition, which effectively dissolved the marriage, not the subsequent decree of the court. Hence no marriage subsisted between the parties at the time of the cohabitation. On appeal by the husband, however, the District Court dismissed the petition for divorce on the ground that it was a settled rule of the traditionally authoritative legal texts that it was the decree of the court which terminated the marriage in these cases, not the wife's mere declaration, and that accordingly her petition must fail because she had consummated the marriage before the effective exercise of the option of puberty. The wife's appeal to the High Court against this decision was opposed by the husband on the principal ground that the court of first instance had acted without authority in departing from a settled rule of Muslim law. It was this central issue which, following Pakistani procedure, was referred to the full bench of the High Court, the precise terms of the question formulated being: "Can courts differ from the views of imams and other jurisconsults of Muslim Law [that is, the doctrine of the authoritative legal manuals] on grounds of public policy, justice, equity, and good conscience?"

The question was answered in a judgment which ran to almost 30,000 words and amounted, in its own admission, to a survey of "the vast subject of Muslim jurisprudence; by no means an easy task even for the most learned in this science, and undoubtedly the most difficult assignment undertaken by the members of the Bench."

However, with one dissent, the Bench boldy affirmed that "if there is no clear rule of decision in Qur'anic and traditional text [that is, the *sunna*] . . . a court may resort to private reasoning and, in that, will undoubtedly be guided by the rules of justice, equity, and good conscience. . . . The views of the earlier jurists and imams are entitled to the utmost respect and cannot be lightly disturbed; but the right to differ from them must not be denied to the present-day courts." These statements amount to a renunciation of the doctrine of *taqlīd* in the widest possible sense. The courts of today are no longer bound to adhere either to the substantive doctrines of the traditional authorities or to the principles of juristic reasoning upon which they were formally based. For the concept of "justice, equity, and good conscience" is clearly of very much wider scope than the basic classical principle of analogical deduction (*qiyās*). In a way it represents a return to the freedom of juristic speculation which was enjoyed by the earliest jurists of Islam under the name of *ra'y*.

In sum, then, the essential difference between traditional and modern legal philosophy is that a social practice or institution can find its justification in the traditional view only by the positive support of divine revelation, but in the modern view by the absence of any negative precept of divine revelation. Law may be legitimately founded upon and generated by social needs provided it does not infringe the limits set by the divine command.

Along with this change in jurisprudential thought, from its traditional attitude of detached idealism to a functional approach to the question of law in society, has come a different view of the role of the courts charged with the application of the law. Traditionally the *qāḍī* was hidebound, not only by the rigid system of procedure and evidence, but also by the precise and detailed complex of legal rules in the authoritative manuals which left him little or no room for personal initiative. Today, however, the tendency is to vest a much wider discretion in the courts applying Sharī'a law to deal with the problems of society, so that they now assume, to a much greater extent then hitherto, the responsibility of organs of real social purpose.

In matrimonial issues the courts in Middle Eastern countries are now playing an increasingly active role as custodians of the religious and social ethic of contemporary Islam. Permission of the court is now often a prerequisite of a marriage contract. Such permission may be refused in Syria and Jordan, for example, if there is such a difference between the ages of the husband and wife as to make the proposed union undesirable in the court's opinion. So, too, in giving permission for a polygamous marriage the courts in Syria are required to be satisfied that the husband is financially able to provide proper maintenance and support for a plurality of wives. In Iraq the courts must also be satisfied that there is "some lawful benefit involved" in a proposed polygamous union, and may refuse their permission "if any failure of equal treatment between co-wives is feared." In the case of a husband exercising his power to divorce his wife by repudiation the courts now have a discretionary power to award the wife suitable compensation in Tunisia, Syria, and, to a lesser degree, in Morocco.

But perhaps the clearest illustration of this greater and more personal responsibility of the courts today lies in the law relating to the custody of young children following the estrangement or divorce of their parents.

Under traditional Sharīʿa law the father, or, failing him, some other close male agnate relative, is the proper guardian of the minor child's person. He has the right to control the upbringing and education of the child, and upon him falls the duty of its maintenance and support. But the bare right to the custody of children (known as *ḥaḍāna*), following the separation of the parents, belongs to the mother. This right is subject to certain conditions—inter alia, that the mother is a trustworthy person, that her place of residence is within accessible reach of the father or other guardian of the person, and that she does not remarry. The mother's right of custody lasts, under Ḥanafī law, until boys reach the age of seven and girls the age of nine; and with the termination of the period of *ḥaḍāna*, custody of the young person generally passes to the father.

In disputes concerning the custody of children the duty of the traditional *qāḍī*'s tribunal was simply to apply these rigid rules which viewed *ḥaḍāna* essentially as a right belonging to the child's mother. But modern law places the emphasis upon *ḥaḍāna* as a duty to be exercised in the best interests of the child, and allows the court a much greater discretion to implement this principle. Thus the Explanatory Memorandum to an Egyptian law of 1929 commented that "the public welfare requires that the court should have liberty to decide what is of most benefit to a boy after the age of seven and a girl after the age of nine." And the law accordingly enacted that "the *qāḍī* may give permission for women's right to the custody of a boy to be extended from the age of seven up to nine, and of a girl from the age of nine up to eleven, if it appears that their welfare so requires." In 1932 the Sudan further extended the court's discretion in this regard up to puberty for boys and the commencement of married life for girls. The Syrian law of 1953 significantly recognizes that the father may, in certain circumstances, be the more proper custodian of his minor children than female relatives other than the mother when it provides: "If a wife deserts her husband, and her children are more than five years old, the *qāḍī* may place them with whichever of the spouses he sees fit, provided he has regard to the welfare of the children." So, too, the Tunisian law of 1957 expressly provides that the best interests of the child are to take precedence over the strict rules of the traditional law in a number of different particulars; while the Iraqi law of 1961 states that any dispute regarding custody shall be decided by the *qāḍī* "in the interests of the child," and that the *qāḍī* may extend the mother's right of custody beyond the usual age "if it appears that the interests of the child so require."

A similar approach to problems of custody has been adopted by the courts in Pakistan. In *Zohra Begum* v. *Latif Ahmad Munawwar*, 1965, the facts were that the appellant wife, after two years of marriage during which two children were born, had left the respondent husband to go and live with her parents. Eight years passed, during which time the husband had never seen his wife or children or made any contribution toward their maintenance, and then the husband divorced the wife by *ṭalāq*. This led to prolonged litigation concerning the wife's dower and a claim by the wife for maintenance for the children. Eventually the husband applied for custody of the children, a boy now aged eight and a girl aged nine.

Following the rules relating to the duration of the mother's right of custody as laid down in the traditional authorities, the court of first instance allowed the mother to retain custody of the girl but ordered that the boy be handed over to the father. The High Court of Lahore, however, allowed the mother's appeal against this order and granted her continuing custody of both her children. If custody were to be granted to the father, declared the court, the children would "find themselves more or less choked in the custody of a stranger who has had such a long-drawn and bitter litigation with their mother. In the circumstances it is likely that if they are removed from the affection of their mother, their emotional and mental growth may be retarded. The plea raised [by the father] was a counterblast to the civil suit instituted [by the mother] against him rather than motivated by a sudden outburst of affection for the welfare of the minors."

So, too, in *Bharai* v. *Wazir Muhammad*, 1966, the High Court rejected the strict rule of traditional Ḥanafī law that a divorced mother forfeits her right to the custody of her minor daughter if she remarries, and refused to grant a father's application for the custody of his minor daughter who had lived with the mother since the parents' divorce, despite the fact that the mother had remarried. The best prospect for a happy life for the child, the court observed, lay in her remaining with the mother. "It is not possible to get rid of the impression that [the father] applied for the custody of [the child] not out of any love or compassion for her but merely to avoid execution of the maintenance order that had been made [in favor of the child] against him."

Notwithstanding the achievements of the reform movement to date, however, it would be wholly wrong to suppose that these have met with general approval or that any Muslim government has yet a mandate to proceed full ahead along the course of what the modernists would describe as social progress. There is still a deep-rooted opposition to change both in principle and in practice.

On the theoretical level conservative elements roundly condemn the new liberalism in legal thought as un-Islamic. They see it, not merely as an undesirable and unnecessary departure from the status quo, but as a process of secularization of the law. The impetus behind the reforms, they claim, is simply a desire to adopt the standards and values of Western civilization, and the claim of reinterpreting the Qur'ān is a mere device to achieve this preconceived purpose. So to allow social aims to fashion the terms of the law is a direct contradiction of the fundamental principle of Islam that it is for society to conform to the terms of the divine law objectively determined. It is therefore a process which ultimately must undermine the very roots of the religious faith itself.

It was conservative opposition of this kind, it may be recalled, that prevented the implementation of the proposals made by the Pakistani Commission on Family Law that a husband should be forced to provide suitable maintenance and support for a wife he has repudiated. It is also noteworthy that the Iraqi Law of Personal Status promulgated in 1959 lacks any provision for compensation for divorced wives. And even the most recent, and certainly the most radical, piece of modernist legislation in Islam, the Family Protection Act promulgated in Iran in 1967, contains an interesting concession to conservative sentiment. This act took the unprecedented step of abolishing altogether the husband's power of *ṭalāq*. In brief, divorce can now take place in Iran only when a spouse establishes to the satisfaction of the court that one of the grounds for divorce, as specified by the act, exists. In this the husband and wife stand on an exact parity. Under the traditional Sharī'a law as applied in Iran, of course, the spouses were far from being on an equal footing in the matter of effecting divorce. *Ṭalāq* was the prerogative of the husband, and the spouses could only be put on a footing of equality if the husband desired this and was prepared to delegate his power of *ṭalāq* to the wife. It was this traditional institution of a delegated power of divorce which was ostensibly invoked by the framers of the Family Protection Act as the basis for their reform. For the act states, in sum, that marriage contracts henceforth must contain a compulsory agreement under which the husband authorizes the wife to apply to the court for a divorce in specified circumstances; and these circumstances are precisely the grounds of divorce laid down by the act. In short, the radical reform of putting the spouses on a parity in the matter of divorce was expressed in terms calculated to cause the minimum of offense to traditionalist views of divorce.

In the matter of the practical effect of the reforms embodied in the modernist legislation the attitude of the courts, is, of course, decisive. This is particularly true of the Middle Eastern codes because of their remarkable brevity and the consequent latitude of interpretation which is allowed to the court. Moreover, as I have observed, the codes contain many general propositions deliberately designed to give the judge a broad discretion in the application of the law. Here it must be admitted that the terms of the codes often appear to have been designed by and for an urban elite and to be out of line with the more conservative temper of the mass of the population as a whole. Hence the courts, either through personal inclination or through a deliberate policy of catering for the prevailing social climate, may not always have given to the codes the practical effect, or may not have applied them in the spirit, that their authors would have desired. In Syria, for example, the courts seem generally reluctant to decide that a husband's repudiation of his wife is "harmful" to her to the degree that would entitle her to compensation. In Tunisia, the power of the court to award compensation to wives whose husbands have insisted on repudiating them has been used most sparingly. Finally, the courts in Iraq have made little use of their new power to grant a wife a divorce on the ground of "harm" caused to her by the husband—a term which has been very narrowly construed. In one case an Iraqi court decided that such "harm" did not exist where the husband persistently accused his wife of adultery, notwithstanding the fact that in the Iraqi locality concerned such an accusation would normally put the wife in peril of her life from the vengeance of her own relatives attempting to stamp out the disgrace brought upon the family.

In universal legal history there can hardly have been any more resounding clash between the forces of stability and the impetus for change than that which has confronted contemporary Islam. Stability lay in the fortress of the Sharīʿa doctrine recorded in the medieval legal manuals which represented, for each school, the universally and eternally valid system of the divine law, and which, as an expression of the ideal system of Islamic behavior, had enjoyed a paramount and exclusive authority of more than ten centuries' standing. Under the shock of attack from the forces of change—the social and economic needs of Muslim society today as conceived by the reformers—this fortress has crumbled. Parts of it, like the commercial and the criminal law, have been almost completely destroyed. But the area of family law still holds out, thanks to a process of redeployment and reconstruction of its defenses. By utilizing doctrines from other schools, by freeing the judges and jurists from the authoritarian doctrine of *taqlīd* and allowing a greater freedom of juristic reasoning both in the interpretation of divine revelation and in the solution of problems not specifically regulated therein, Sharīʿa law has retained its control over family life and in some cases reasserted that control with a new vigor through a resurgence of legal moralism.

If I may be permitted to continue the military metaphor, this conflict came upon Islam with a pressure and a rapidity of events which necessitated immediate tactical maneuvers and did not allow for long-term strategic planning. Islamic jurisprudence has succeeded, by what are essentially ad hoc measures, in solving the immediate problems of family law, but it has not yet evolved any firm or systematic principles to ensure that it is equipped to deal with future developments. There are many conflicts still unresolved, many problems unanswered. And yet, in this still transitional stage, one fact stands out in bold relief. The attitude of detached idealism which dominated the science of Sharī'a law in the past seems gone for ever. Muslim jurisprudence today is squarely facing the task of regulating the needs and aspirations of human life. It is a science of social purpose. It is this which constitutes the present real achievement of Muslim jurisprudence and which must provide its continuing inspiration for the future.

# INDEX


Abū Ḥanīfa, 21
Abū Yūsuf, 60
*'Adāla*, 62
*Aga Mahomed* v. *Koolsom Beebee*, 50
Aḥmad b. Hanbal, 22
Ahmadu Bello University, 100–101
*Al-Muwṭṭa'*, 60
Analogy, 6, 17, 19, 23

*Balquis Fatima* v. *Najm-ul-ikran Qureshi*, 53
Bequests, 86–87
*Bharai* v. *Wazir Muhammad*, 111

Codification, 35–36, 38–39, 99–100
Commercial law, 91, 100
Consensus, 23
Criminal law, 91, 100, 103–4
Custody of children, 109–12
Customary law, 4, 10, 11, 12, 13, 19, 28, 32

Dissolution of Muslim Marriages Act, 51
Divorce: by judicial decree, 2, 30, 36, 45, 48, 51, 82, 114; by *khul'*, 53–55; by mutual consent, 45; by *ṭalāq*, 45, 46, 47, 52, 83, 85, 89–90, 92, 113
Documentary evidence, 73–74
Donkey, Case of the, 15–17

Egypt, 72, 94, 98, 99, 109
Equity, 17, 19
European law, 72
Evidence, 61–66

Family Protection Act, 113
Family settlements, 88–89
Fornication, 62, 65, 78

Habīb Bū Ruqayba, 102
*Ḥaḍāna*, 109–12
*Ḥadīth*, 5, 6
*Ḥanafīs*, 21
*Ḥanbalīs*, 21
*Ḥiyal*, 87–91
Homicide, 62, 72

*Ibāḥa*, 29–30, 103
Ibn Qudāma, 33
Ibn Taymiyya, 34
*'Idda*, 46
*Ijmā'*, 22, 23
*Ijtihād*, 41, 42, 43, 48, 96
India, 49
Inheritance, 7–19, 31–33, 89, 94, 98–99, 104–5
Iqbāl, 44
Iran, 113
Iraq, 37–38, 93, 98, 108, 114; Law of Personal Status, 113
*Istiḥsān*, 7, 17
*Istiṣlāḥ*, 7

Jordan, 108

*Khamessa*, 70–71
*Khurshid Bibi* v. *Mohamed Amin*, 56
*Khurshid Jan* v. *Fazal Dad*, 105–7

Legal education, 100
Legal stratagems, 87–91
Lybia, 72

Mālik b. Anas, 14, 21, 60, 81
Mālik's Rule, 9, 18–19
Majority, 25–26
Marriage: conditions in contract of, 28, 36; court's permission for, 108; guardianship in, 25–27, 35, 36, 83; temporary, 31, 86
Marital relations, 28–30
*Maẓālim* jurisdiction, 66–69
*Metropolitan Properties Co. Ltd.* v. *Purdy*, 40
Morocco, 2, 94, 108
*Muftī*, 84
*Mughnī*, 33
Muḥammad Abdūh, 44
*Muhammad Ibrahim* v. *Ghulam Ahmad*, 35
*Muḥtasib*, 84
*Mujtahid*, 41
*Muqallid*, 43

Obligatory bequests, 94–95, 105
Option of puberty, 105–6

Pakistan, 49–56, 104, 110; Muslim Family Laws Ordinance, 51, 104–5
Paternity, 74–75, 93–94
Polygamy, 28, 30, 93–94, 102
Privy Council, 50
Procedure, 61–66

*Qāḍī*, 40, 57, 58–60, 61, 66, 99, 108
Qayrawan, 58
*Qiyās*, 6, 107
Qur'ān: legal regulations of, 2, 10, 11, 48, 49, 50, 80, 84, 103

*Ra'y*, 4, 5, 6, 22, 107
*Ribā*, 69–71, 87–88

Sa'd's Case, 10–11
*Saleh* v. *Odhams Press*, 26–27
Sexual morality, 78–79
Shāfi'ī, 6, 21, 22, 42
*Shaw* v. *the Director of Public Prosecutions*, 77
Shī'ī law, 31–33
*Siyāsa*, 68–69, 73, 101
Sudan, 72, 98, 110
*Sunna*, 4, 6, 23, 41, 93
Sunnī schools, 21–22, 24, 34–35
Syria, 94, 108, 114; Law of Personal Status, 36, 46–48, 92, 110

*Taḥlīl*, 90
*Taqlīd*, 43, 50, 56, 96, 107
Tunisia, 36, 94, 98, 99, 102, 108, 114; Law of Personal Status, 36, 48, 92, 94, 102, 110
Turkey, 101

Umar, 15, 16
*Uṣūl al-fiqh*, 3
Usury, 70, 87–88

*Waqf*, 88–89

*Zinā*, 62, 78
*Zohra Begum* v. *Latif Ahmad Munawwar*, 110